POSTER COLLECTION
NIKLAUS TROXLER

34

Herausgegeben von / Edited by Bettina Richter

Essay von / by Daniel Martin Feige

T0347765

MUSEUM FÜR GESTALTUNG ZÜRICH
PLAKATSAMMLUNG / POSTER COLLECTION

LARS MÜLLER PUBLISHERS

1 **McCoy Tyner Sextet**
1980

Nur wenige Gestalterinnen und Gestalter der Gegenwart widmen sich dem Medium Plakat noch mit solcher Ausdauer wie Niklaus Troxler. Selbst wenn die Gestaltung von CD-, LP- und Buch-Covern, von Logos, von grafischen Innen- und Aussenraumge-staltungen ebenso wie freie illustrative und künstlerische Arbeiten zu seinem umfang-reichen Œuvre zählen, gilt dem Plakat seine Leidenschaft – insbesondere dem Jazz-plakat. 1966 organisierte Troxler das erste Jazzkonzert in Willisau, 1975 gründete er ebendort ein Festival, das seither jedes Jahr etablierte und weniger bekannte Namen des Schweizer und internationalen Jazz auf die Bühne bringt. Bis 2009 leitete er die Veranstaltung und war für die Gestaltung der Konzert- und Festivalplakate verantwort-lich, dann gab er beides an eine jüngere Generation ab.

Mit seinem Schaffen setzt sich Troxler über alle vermeintlichen Regeln «guter Gestal-tung» hinweg, die seit den 1950er-Jahren die Schweizer Grafik auf den Swiss Style reduzieren. Orientieren sich seine frühen Jazzplakate noch stark an einer figurativen Verständlichkeit und porträtieren Musikerinnen und Musiker sowie die klassischen Instrumente des Jazz mit verspieltem Witz und versteckten Bilderrätseln, so emanzi-piert sich Troxler bald von jeder Narration. Sein virtuoses Spiel in der Fläche imitiert den Charakter der experimentellen Musik und nimmt deren Improvisationsgesten auf. Troxlers Plakate sind synästhetische Ereignisse und machen Musik physisch erfahr-bar. Der fiebrig-nervöse Strich einzelner Entwürfe holt das Zeitmoment in die Gestal-tung, andere Plakate sprengen die Zweidimensionalität. Neugierig und offen für tech-nische Neuerungen, bezieht Troxler ab Mitte der 1990er-Jahre die Möglichkeiten des Computers in den kreativen Prozess ein, ohne dabei seine Handmade-Ästhetik preis-zugeben. Troxlers Kosmos manifestiert sich auch im Erfindungsreichtum von Schrift und Typografie. Immer wieder auf neue Weise und mit anderen Mitteln entwirft, skiz-ziert, kleckst, malt, tippt, stempelt Troxler Schriften, schichtet, verschränkt, konstruiert und dekonstruiert Lettern – und lotet so die Grenzen der Lesbarkeit aus.

Anlässlich von Niklaus Troxlers 75. Geburtstag vereint der vorliegende Band neben ausgewählten Jazzplakaten auch Theater- und Ausstellungsplakate sowie Arbeiten für klassische Schweizer Auftraggeber wie die Olma, den Genfer Autosalon oder den Nationalzirkus Knie und wirft ein Schlaglicht auf Troxlers gesellschaftspolitische Plakate. In der Gesamtschau zeigt sich bei aller entwerferischen Vielfalt eine klare Haltung: Im lustvollen Spiel mit den technischen Möglichkeiten ebenso wie mit unter-schiedlichen gestalterischen Zugriffen – die kompakte Form, der unruhige Strich, die definierte Linie, die leuchtende Farbigkeit, die strenge Farbreduktion –, im Durchdekli-nieren gleicher Motive, die mit wechselnder Bedeutung auftreten, erfindet sich Troxler stets neu und bleibt sich dennoch treu.

Bettina Richter

PREFACE

Few contemporary designers devote themselves to the poster medium with such perseverance as Niklaus Troxler. His extensive oeuvre includes the design of CD, album, and book covers, logos, interior and exterior graphics, as well as free illustrative and artistic works. However, the poster—and especially the jazz poster—is his passion. Troxler organized the first jazz concert in Willisau in 1966, and in 1975 he founded a festival there that has since brought established and lesser-known names in Swiss and international jazz to the stage on an annual basis. He directed the event and was responsible for the design of the concert and festival posters until 2009, at which time he handed both over to a younger generation.

Troxler's work defies all the supposed rules of "good design" that have reduced Swiss graphic design to the Swiss Style since the 1950s. While his early jazz posters were still strongly oriented toward figurative comprehensibility, portraying musicians and the traditional instruments of jazz using playful wit and hidden pictorial riddles, he soon emancipated himself entirely from any narrative. His virtuoso play with surfaces imitates the character of experimental music and adopts its improvisational gestures. His posters are synesthetic events and make music physically tangible. Feverishly nervous strokes bring the element of time into the individual designs, while other posters go beyond two-dimensionality. From the mid-1990s on, curious and open to technical innovations, Troxler incorporated the possibilities of the computer into the creative process without abandoning his handmade aesthetics. A characteristic feature of his cosmos is the inventiveness of typeface and typography. Again and again, in new ways and with different means, Troxler designs, sketches, blots, paints, types, and stamps typefaces, layers, interlaces, constructs, and deconstructs letters, thus exploring the limits of legibility.

Published on the occasion of Niklaus Troxler's 75th birthday, this volume brings together selected jazz posters, theater and exhibition posters, as well as works for classic Swiss clients such as the Olma Agriculture and Dairy Fair, the Geneva Motor Show, and the national Knie Circus. It also spotlights Troxler's sociopolitical posters. For all the diversity of his designs, a consistent vision is apparent everywhere: by playing with technical possibilities and different creative approaches—the compact form, the restless stroke, the defined line, the luminous colorfulness, the strict reduction of color—and by reinterpreting the same motifs, which appear with changing meaning, Troxler is in a constant process of reinvention while always remaining true to himself.

Bettina Richter

2 **Ellery Eskelin / Christian Weber / Michael Griener**
2019

3 **Jazz Festival Willisau 2000**
2000

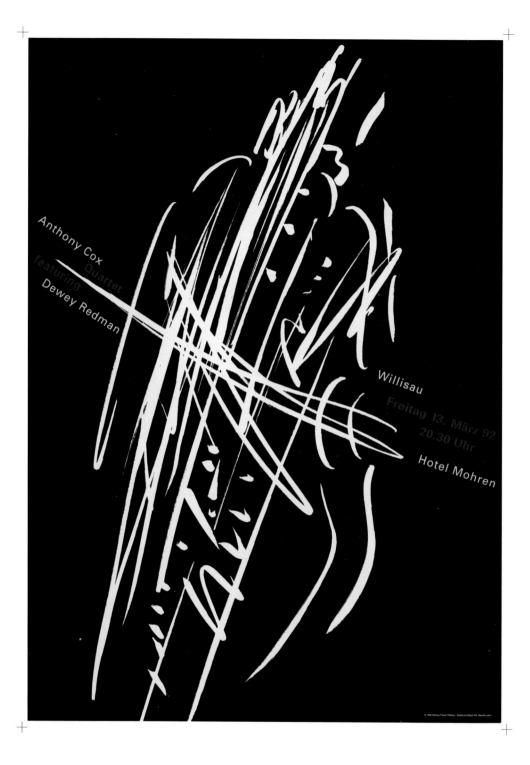

4 **Anthony Cox Quartet Featuring Dewey Redman**
1992

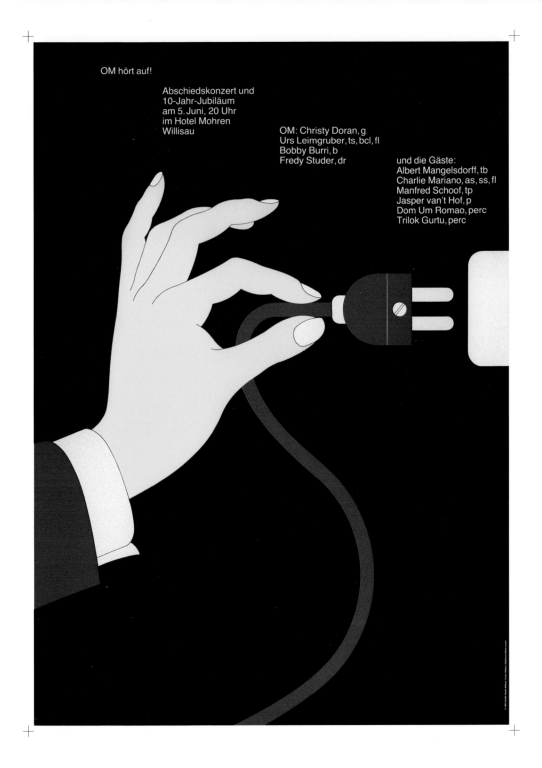

OM hört auf!

Abschiedskonzert und
10-Jahr-Jubiläum
am 5. Juni, 20 Uhr
im Hotel Mohren
Willisau

OM: Christy Doran, g
Urs Leimgruber, ts, bcl, fl
Bobby Burri, b
Fredy Studer, dr

und die Gäste:
Albert Mangelsdorff, tb
Charlie Mariano, as, ss, fl
Manfred Schoof, tp
Jasper van't Hof, p
Dom Um Romao, perc
Trilok Gurtu, perc

5 **OM hört auf!**
1982

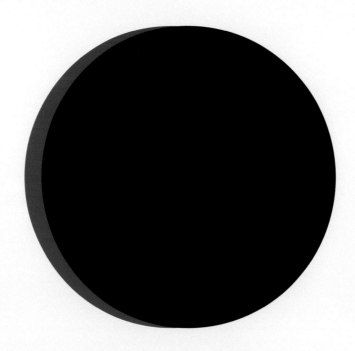

Missing Fukuda

Shigeo Fukuda 1932-2009. Poster for the Fukuda Memorial Exhibitions in Haneshi and Tokyo by Niklaus Troxler

6 **Missing Fukuda**
2010

7 **[Tote Bäume – Dead Trees]**
1992

JAZZ FÜRS AUGE:
ZUR ÄSTHETIK DER PLAKATGESTALTUNG NIKLAUS TROXLERS

Daniel Martin Feige

In der Jazzmusik werden unter den Schlagworten *ahead* und *laid back* Spielweisen bezeichnet, die leicht vor oder hinter dem Beat sind. Sie sind nicht zuletzt dafür verantwortlich, dass der Jazz seine eigenwillige, rhythmisch treibende Kraft entwickelt und eine Musik ist, in der mit jedem Zug ihr ganzes Gelingen auf dem Spiel steht. Die *time* und das Timing dürfen dabei nicht verloren gehen, denn sonst verliert auch das entsprechende Umspielen und Bespielen des Beats seinen Sinn. In abgewandelter Weise gilt dieses Diktum selbst noch für die offenen Formen des Free Jazz, bei dem die Spielzüge der Musikerinnen und Musiker ebenfalls passend sein können oder nicht.

Diese Bemerkung zur rhythmischen Gestaltung des Jazz steht nicht nur deshalb am Anfang, weil der Jazz wie sicher keine andere Kunstform die Arbeiten Niklaus Troxlers geprägt hat. Sie dient vielmehr auch als Einstieg, weil im Jazz nicht allein etwas *on spot* sein oder leicht danebengehen kann, sondern der Jazz eine bestimmte Zeit und ein Lebensgefühl treffen oder verpassen kann. Das gilt auch für Plakate und ganz besonders für Troxlers Plakate: Sie bringen ihre Themen und ihre Zeit in verdichteter Weise auf den Punkt.

EINE VISUELLE GESCHICHTE DES JAZZ

Gerade die Jazzplakate von Troxler für das 1975 von ihm begründete Jazzfestival Willisau, dessen Rolle für die Distribution und mittelbar auch für die Entwicklung des Jazz in Europa nicht unterschätzt werden darf, sind zentraler Bestandteil einer visuellen Geschichte des Jazz geworden. Die grafische Dimension mag im Jazz weniger ausgeprägt sein als in der Popmusik, die, wie Diedrich Diederichsen überzeugend gezeigt hat,[1] gar nicht ausschliesslich Musik, sondern ein Komplex von Musik, Covern, Mode, Posen und so fort ist. Aber auch für den Jazz sind grafische und bildliche Aspekte keineswegs irrelevant. Neben den ikonischen Fotografien von Francis Wolff für Blue Note müssen aus europäischer Perspektive auch die Plakate Troxlers genannt werden: Sie haben dem Jazz ein spezifisches Gesicht gegeben.

Die Nähe zum Jazz geht darüber hinaus, dass diese Musik für Troxler Anlass und Sujet vieler Arbeiten ist. Im Folgenden möchte ich den Versuch unternehmen, seine Plakate selbst als Ausdruck einer musikalischen Logik zu lesen. Handelt es sich doch bei der Plakatkunst (wie trotz anderslautender puristischer Bekundungen in Wahrheit bei allen Künsten) um eine ästhetische Form, die in vielfältiger Weise von anderen Künsten informiert ist und damit in einem intermedialen Zusammenhang verschiedener ästhetischer Medien betrachtet werden muss. Der zentrale Gedanke, den ich mit Blick auf einige der gezeigten Plakate entwickle, lautet dabei: Es ist keine kontingente Tatsache und keine schlicht biografische Information, dass Troxler oft Plakate gestaltet hat, die

---

1 Vgl. Diedrich Diederichsen, «Einführung», in: ders., *Über Pop-Musik,* Köln 2014.

sich dem Jazz widmen. Vielmehr hat seine grafische Sprache eine grosse Affinität zu dieser Musik, sodass der Konnex Jazz und Grafikdesign, den ich hier als Zugang wähle, ein zentraler Schlüssel zum Verständnis seiner Arbeiten sein kann. Troxlers Plakate sind Jazz fürs Auge.

DAS PLAKAT ALS DISZIPLIN DES GRAFIKDESIGNS

Design und Jazz haben dabei gerade unter der Ägide eines herkömmlichen Verständnisses der Künste eine zentrale Gemeinsamkeit: Sie sind quasi illegitime Künste, Grenzkünste. Noch bis vor wenigen Dekaden musste man lesen, dass der Jazz gegenüber der Musik in der Tradition europäischer Kunstmusik ästhetisch ärmer sei,[2] weil er wegen seines improvisatorischen Charakters nicht die Komplexität von Orchesterkompositionen von der Wiener Klassik bis zur Spätromantik gewinnen könne. Das Plakat wiederum ist oft aus dem Diskurs der Kunst ausgeschlossen worden, da es gegenüber paradigmatischen Werken der Malerei offenkundig zumeist einen funktionalen Charakter hat. Solche Thesen sind problematisch, weil sie an die entsprechenden Gegenstände Kriterien anlegen, die ihnen unangemessen sind. Zugleich drängt sich die Frage auf: Gehört das Plakat nicht in den Bereich des Designs anstatt in denjenigen der Künste? Trotz der in der Gegenwart vielfältigen Entgrenzungen beider Sphären gilt, dass die Unterscheidung von Kunst und Design wichtig ist und nicht vorschnell aufgegeben werden sollte. Ein Plakat, das ein potenzielles Publikum über ein anstehendes Konzert informiert, ist nicht dasselbe wie ein Gemälde, das um der Erfahrung selbst willen betrachtet werden will. Auch wenn ein Plakat mit derselben Haltung angeschaut werden kann wie ein abstraktes Gemälde, wird es nicht dadurch schon eines.

Die Unterscheidung von Kunst und Design ist ohnehin nur dann problematisch, wenn sie als Wertung im Sinne einer hierarchischen Unterscheidung verstanden wird.[3] Der Begriff der angewandten Kunst wurde oftmals so expliziert, dass die angewandten Künste qua des Angewandten ästhetisch weniger relevant oder wertvoll seien als die freien Künste. Dabei handelt es sich um einen Trugschluss.[4] Das Plakat als Disziplin des Grafikdesigns lässt sich also als Bereich ästhetischer Gegenstände und als spezifische ästhetische Form begreifen, die auch dann, wenn sie nicht zu den schönen Künsten gezählt wird, von deren Aspekten vielfältig beeinflusst und ihnen keineswegs in Relevanz und Wert unterzuordnen ist. Das Plakat ist eine ästhetische Praxis eigener Art – und gerade hier zeigt das Grafikdesign in ausgeprägter Weise, wie die Geschichte der bildenden Kunst auch funktionale Gegenstände informiert hat.

DIE MUSIKALITÄT DER PLAKATE

In welcher Weise lässt sich vor diesem Hintergrund die spezifische Nähe der grafischen Sprache von Troxlers Plakaten zum Jazz konkretisieren? Sie ist jedenfalls nicht so zu verstehen, dass sie das dem Jazz manchmal (und oft fälschlich) zugeschriebene Moment des Rauschhaften exemplifiziert; beispielhaft kann man hier im europäischen

2 Paradigmatisch ist hier die von Philip Alperson in seinem kanonischen Text zur musikalischen Improvisation kolportierte Bemerkung Denis Duttons; vgl. Philip Alperson, «On Musical Improvisation», in: *The Journal of Aesthetics and Art Criticism* 43 (1984), S. 17–29, hier: S. 22.
3 Vgl. zur systematischen Entwicklung dieser Überlegungen auch Daniel Martin Feige, *Design. Eine philosophische Analyse,* Berlin 2018, v. a. Kapitel 4.

Jazz an Peter Brötzmanns *Machine Gun* denken oder im amerikanischen Jazz an die späten Alben John Coltranes mit ihrer ins Mystische überhöhten Religiosität. Die Bildsprache Troxlers ist gegenüber solchen Beschreibungen gedämpfter und zurückhaltender, ihre Verwandtschaft zum Jazz soll nachfolgend paradigmatisch anhand interpretativer Bemerkungen zu einigen seiner Plakate aufgezeigt werden.

Beginnen wir mit einem Blick auf einen echten Klassiker: das Plakat zum Konzert des McCoy Tyner Sextets von 1980 1. Das Spiel von Vordergrund in Gelb und Hintergrund in Violett und das damit einhergehende Kontrastsehen stellen ein grafisch markantes Verfahren dar, das die Typografie in ihrer räumlichen und bildlichen Dimension durchdekliniert – was ein Signum letztlich allen Grafikdesigns ist, das mit Typografie arbeitet. Das Plakat drückt ausserdem Bewegung aus; die Buchstaben gehen in Kontrasten ineinander über, ohne freilich ihre Kontur zu verlieren. Wenn man Plakate nicht als bloss formales Spiel von Zeichen begreift, sondern so, dass sie in ihrer ästhetischen Gestaltung konkrete Inhalte thematisieren, könnte man weitergehend sagen: Die Dynamik von Vorder- und Hintergrund, von Lesbarkeit und Unlesbarkeit – wenn die Lettern so gesehen werden, dass sie sich in den Farben auflösen – ist eine grafische Interpretation der Dynamik von McCoy Tyners Spielweise, die weniger in herkömmlichen, durch Harmonien vorgegebenen Spannungsbögen denkt als vielmehr in Skalen, die nicht schon selbst bestimmte An- und Entspannungen mit sich bringen. Dasselbe gilt auch für die Interaktion der beteiligten Musikerinnen und Musiker, die charakteristischerweise ebenfalls nach einer Logik funktioniert, in der die Musiker graduell in den Vorder- und Hintergrund treten (man denke etwa an die Begleitung eines Musikers, der ein Solo spielt). So gesehen handelt es sich bei diesem Plakat nicht allein um einen für sich bereits virtuosen grafischen Gegenstand, sondern um eine Arbeit, die tatsächlich etwas von der spezifischen Dynamik ihres Sujets durch die Form der Gestaltung artikuliert.

Auch für das im Premierenjahr des Jazzfestivals Willisau entstandene Plakat zum Konzert von John Abercrombie, Dave Holland und Jack DeJohnette bildet die Arbeit an der Typografie das zentrale Verfahren 40. Anders als im vorangegangenen Beispiel operiert das Plakat aber mit dem Kontrast von hellblauer Typografie und dunkelblauem Untergrund, wobei die Typografie von weissen Flächen durchzogen ist, die gegenständlich gelesen als Wolken erscheinen. Auch hier gibt es ein Spiel von Vorder- und Hintergrund, aber es ist so gestaltet, dass man durch das Plakat gewissermassen hindurchsieht. Die Typografie wird metonymisch verwendet: Sie weist nicht allein auf ein zukünftiges musikalisches Ereignis hin, sondern gewährt auch einen Blick in den Himmel, ins Offene, das für das Spiel der drei Musiker in den 1970er-Jahren charakteristisch war. Durch die unscharf geschnittenen Lettern, die keine gleichförmigen Ränder, sondern allseitig kleine Unebenheiten aufweisen, entwickelt das Plakat dabei eine eigentümliche Dynamik und wirkt trotz seiner statischen Anlage fast kinetisch.

---

4 Er wird ironischerweise von jüngeren Entwicklungen des Social Design, Critical Design und Speculative Design inklusive der beteiligten Diskurse wie Designforschung und Design Thinking mit umgekehrten Vorzeichen wiederholt, wenn hier das Design zur neuen ästhetischen Leitdisziplin ausgerufen wird.

Ein auf den ersten Blick ganz anderes Verfahren wählte Troxler für das 26 Jahre später entstandene Plakat zum Solokonzert David Murrays 59. Es beruht auf einer klaren und auf den ersten Blick einfachen Struktur: kleinere und grössere gelbe und pinke Punkte, die durch gerade Linien miteinander verbunden sind, wobei die Buchstaben in die grösseren Kreise gesetzt sind. Das eigentliche Thema des Plakats bildet aber die Spannung zwischen dieser klaren, fast mechanischen Komposition und der energetischen Spielweise Murrays: Im Sinne eines Aspektwechsels lässt es sich einerseits gegenständlich, andererseits als abstrakte Komposition lesen; dabei ruft es durch die einfache Struktur nicht allein Assoziationen zum Mathematischen, Physikalischen und nicht zuletzt zur Elektrizität auf, sondern erhält durch die genannte Spannung einen dynamischen Charakter, vibriert vor den Augen nahezu. Dass die Affinität zum Jazz nicht allein für solche Plakate gilt, die diesen explizit als Sujet haben, lässt sich exemplarisch anhand des 1991 entstandenen Plakats zum 700-Jahr-Jubiläum der Gründungsurkunde der Schweiz ausweisen 95: Die Übereinstimmung und Differenz der vier gezeichneten Linien operiert zwar mit identifizierbaren Elementen, als Plakat entwickelt es aber gleichermassen einen beweglichen wie improvisatorischen Charakter.

METONYMIE UND METAPHER, WITZ UND VIRTUOSITÄT
Weitere interpretatorische Perspektiven eröffnen sich mit Blick auf Plakate, die eher in einer repräsentationalistischen Weise bildhaft sind. Von Repräsentation zu sprechen meint schlicht, dass Bilder Darstellungen von etwas sein können; nicht alle Bilder exemplifizieren Farben und Formen, sondern viele zeigen Gegenstände, Personen und Situationen. Eine solche gewissermassen semantische Dimension lässt sich nicht unabhängig von der Art und Weise der Gestaltung eines Plakats betrachten, insofern Plakate (das verbindet sie mit Gemälden ebenso wie mit Romanen) nur etwas durch die Art und Weise thematisieren, wie sie es thematisieren. Der amerikanische Kunstphilosoph Arthur C. Danto hat hier treffenderweise darauf hingewiesen, dass die Form der Darstellung selbst als Aspekt des Inhalts verstanden werden muss;[5] man kann sozusagen nicht durch die Gegenstände hindurchsehen auf das, was sie zeigen, sondern muss auf die spezifische Weise ihres Zeigens achtgeben. Diese sinnhafte Dimension im Sinnlichen der Formen, Farben und Flächen wird in Troxlers Plakaten nicht immer und durchweg gemäss des just interpretatorisch ausgewiesenen formalen Spiels von typografischen und räumlichen Eigenarten durchgespielt. Viele Plakate sind durchaus gegenständlicher Art.

So zeigt das 1978 zum Konzert des Anthony Braxton Quartet 15, einem wesentlichen Vertreter des Third Stream, der die Grenze zwischen Jazz und Neuer Musik aufgeweicht hat, eine rätselhafte Landschaft mit verstreuten übergrossen Teilen eines Instruments (oder mehrerer?) und einem Menschen am ebenso übergrossen Saxofon. Das Plakat kann als grafisches Äquivalent der durchaus eigentümlichen Klanglandschaften Braxtons gelesen werden. Don Pullen hingegen spielt nicht nur ein Klavier, die symmetrisch gesetzten Tasten werden zugleich Teil der Stars-and-Stripes-

---

5 Vgl. Arthur C. Danto, *Die Verklärung des Gewöhnlichen. Eine Philosophie der Kunst,* Frankfurt am Main 1991, v. a. Kapitel 6.

Fahne – man kommt nicht umhin, dem Plakat auch eine politische Grammatik zuzuschreiben, wenn die amerikanische Flagge hier aus dem Spiel eines People-of-Color-Musikers räumlich hervorgeht 12.

Vielen dieser eher gegenständlichen Plakate ist zugleich eine enigmatische Qualität eigen. Wird auf dem Plakat zur Ankündigung eines Solokonzerts von Dave Holland 10 der Bass im Sinne einer Synekdoche nahezu zur ganzen Person, ist insbesondere das ikonische Plakat des Cecil-Taylor-Solokonzerts von 1989 in produktiver Weise unentzifferbar 29: ein abgetrennter Finger mit grüner Haut vor schwarzem Hintergrund; ein Objekt, das im Rahmen der psychoanalytischen Theoriebildung innerhalb wie ausserhalb der Ökonomie des Verstehens liegen würde. Aber auch viel visueller Witz findet sich in den Plakaten von Troxler, wenn etwa in jenem zu George Colemans Konzert das Saxofon als Telefon verwendet wird 11 oder sich dasselbe Instrument auf einem anderen Plakat in eine Schlange verwandelt und gewissermassen den Biss der Jazzmusik ausdrückt 18.

DIE PERFORMATIVE DIMENSION DER PLAKATKUNST

Niklaus Troxlers Plakate haben nicht nur eine eigene visuelle Energie, sie beweisen oft visuellen Witz und Virtuosität. Sie im Kontext und Spannungsfeld mit dem Jazz zu lesen, veranschaulicht, dass diese Energie, dieser Witz und die Virtuosität vieles mit gelingenden Jazzimprovisationen gemein haben. Es ist kein Zufall, dass Troxler in jüngster Zeit mit farbigen und schwarzen Klebebändern live in Begleitung von Jazzmusikerinnen und -musikern Wandbilder («Tape Works») erstellt; für eine entsprechende Performance wirbt das Plakat «Tape & Jazz» 104, das selbst mit solchen Klebebändern arbeitet und so typografische wie bildliche und abstrakte Formen entstehen lässt. Diese Praxis stellt eine konsequente Radikalisierung der Sensibilitäten dar, die schon seine frühen Plakate zeigen. In seinen gegenständlichen Bildern ebenso wie seinen die Typografie verräumlichenden Arbeiten nähert sich Troxler dem ungesicherten, offenen und improvisatorischen Charakter des Jazz wie kaum ein zweiter Grafikdesigner an.

Jazz-Crew

Willisau, 30. Sept.
20 Uhr
Hotel Mohren

Frédéric Rabold, tp
Herbert Joos, tp
Walter Huber, bs, s
Bernth Konrad ts, ss
Paul Schwarz, p
Jan Jankeje, b
C. A. Bally, dm

8 **Jazz-Crew**
1973

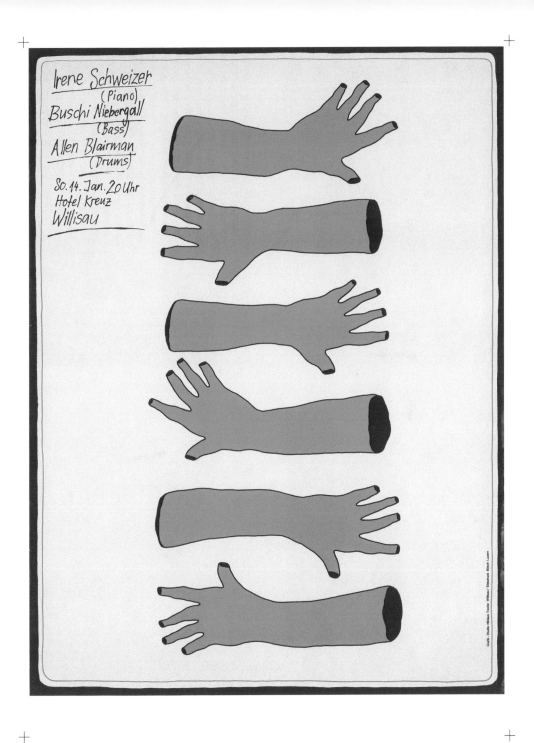

9 **Irène Schweizer / Buschi Niebergall /**
Allen Blairman
1973

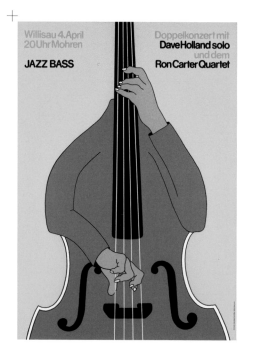

10 **Jazz Bass / Dave Holland Solo /
Ron Carter Quartet**
1981

11 **George Coleman Quartet**
1979

12 **Don Pullen Quartet**
1978

13 **Sun Ra Arkestra**
1980

Chris McGregor p
Dudu Pukwana as
Mike Osborne as
Evan Parker ts,ss
Gary Windo ts
Mongezi Feza tp
Marc Charig tp
Harry Beckett tp
Malcolm Griffiths tb
Nick Evans tb
Radu Malfatti tb
Harry Miller b
Louis Moholo dm

CHRIS
MCGREGOR'S
BROTHERHOOD
OF BREATH

Samstag 27. Januar
20.00 Uhr
Hotel Mohren
Willisau

14 **Chris McGregor's Brotherhood of Breath**
1973

15 **The New Anthony Braxton Quartet**
1978

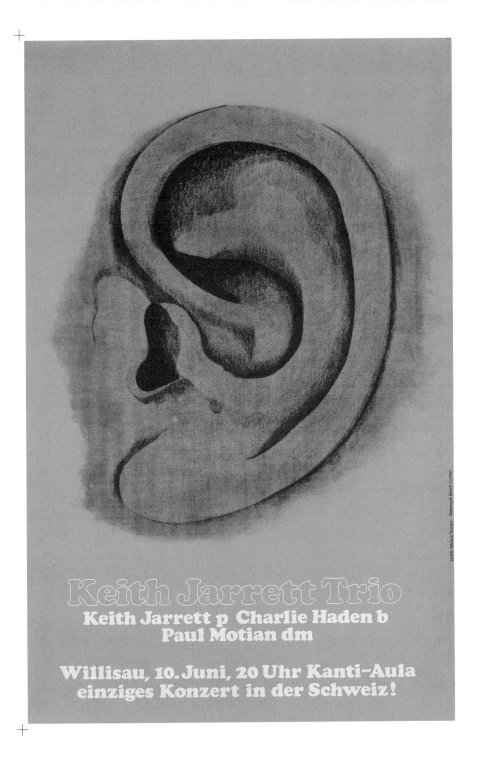

16 **Keith Jarrett Trio**
1972

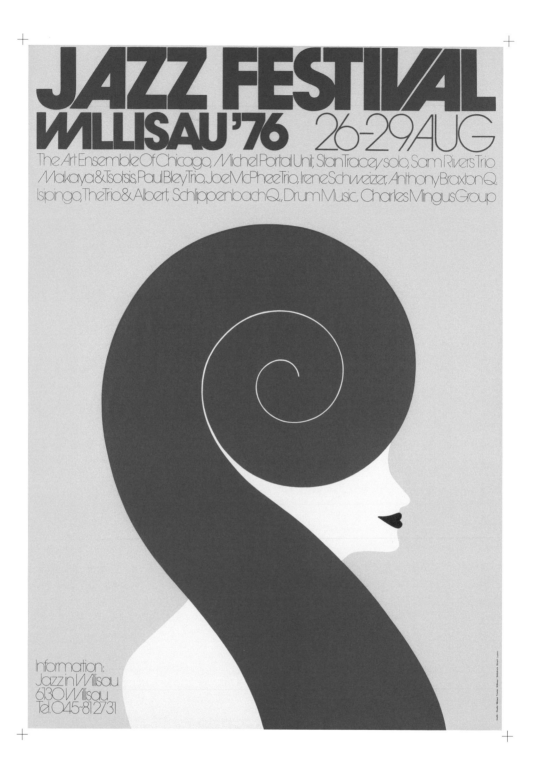

17 Jazz Festival Willisau '76
1976

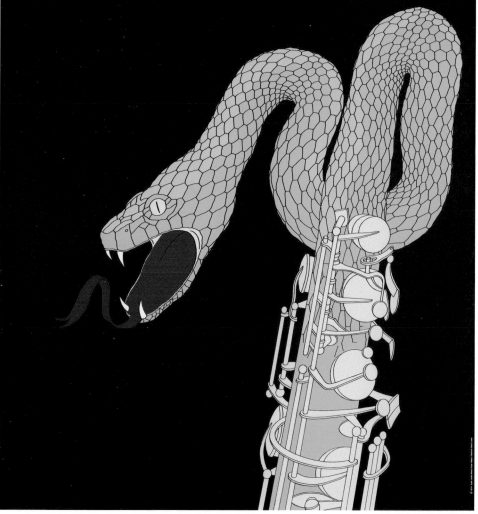

18 **Jazz Festival Willisau '78**
1978

Solo Vocals / Greetje Bijma
2004

Jazz Festival
Willisau '91

29. August – 1. September

Konzert 1: Do 29. Aug. 20.00 h:
BRASIL
Egberto Gismonti · Charlie Haden
Hermeto Pascoal e Grupo

Konzert 2: Fr 30. Aug. 20.00 h:
EAST AND WEST
Walter Zuber Armstrong solo
Samul Nori & Red Sun
Corean Drummer and Dancers
feat. Wolfgang Puschnig, Linda Sharrock
Jamaaladeen Tacuma, Uli Scherer
Bob Stewart First Line Band

Konzert 3: Sa 31. Aug. 14.30 h:
SUPER TRIOS
Carla Bley · Steve Swallow · Andy Sheppard
Geri Allen · Charlie Haden · Paul Motian

Konzert 4: Sa 31. Aug. 20.00 h:
SATURDAY NIGHT SPECIALS
Hans Kennel Alphornquartett
Mani Planzer & Morschachblasorchester
Odean Pope Trio feat.
Gerald Veasely, Cornell Rochester

Konzert 5: So 1. Sept. 14.30 h:
EUROPAMERICA
Irene Schweizer & London
Jazz Composer's Orchestra
Bobby Previte & Empty Suits

Konzert 6: So 1. Sept. 20.00 h:
GREAT GUITARS
Ralph Towner & Oregon
John Scofield Quartet

Konzerte in der Festhalle Willisau
Gratis Camping

Im Zelt:
Do 29. Aug. 18.00 h: Urgent Feel
Fr 30. Aug. 18.00 h: Jazz Dazz Big Band
Sa 31. Aug. 12.00 h: Fun Horns
So 1. Sept. 12.00 h: New Point

Information:
Jazz in Willisau, Postfach, CH-6130 Willisau
Tel. 045-81 27 31

20 **Jazz Festival Willisau '91**
1991

21 **Lucien Dubuis Trio**
2010

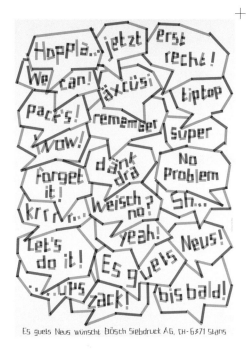

22 **Ellery Eskelin / Han Bennink**
2000

23 **Jazz Italia / Carlo Actis Dato Quartet**
2000

24 **Es guets Neus wünscht Bösch Siebdruck AG**
2008

25 **Marty Ehrlich Quartet N. Y.**
2006

26 **Kölner Saxophon Mafia**
1999

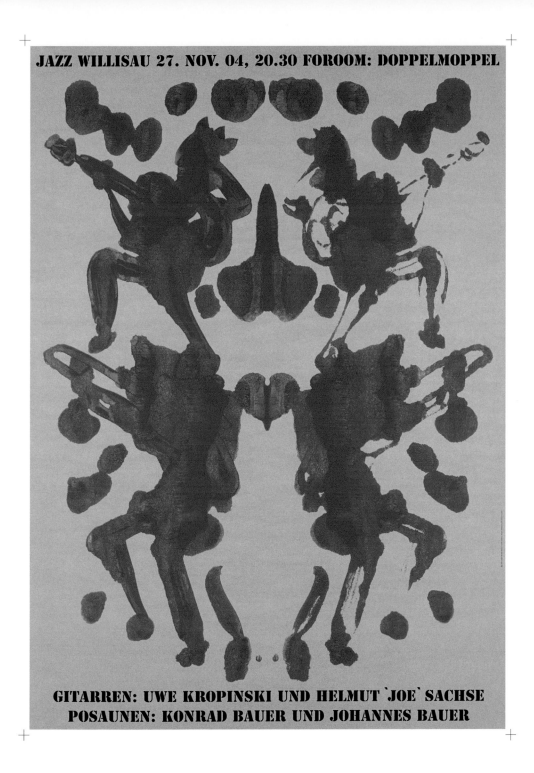

JAZZ WILLISAU 27. NOV. 04, 20.30 FOROOM: DOPPELMOPPEL

GITARREN: UWE KROPINSKI UND HELMUT `JOE` SACHSE
POSAUNEN: KONRAD BAUER UND JOHANNES BAUER

27 **Doppelmoppel**
2004

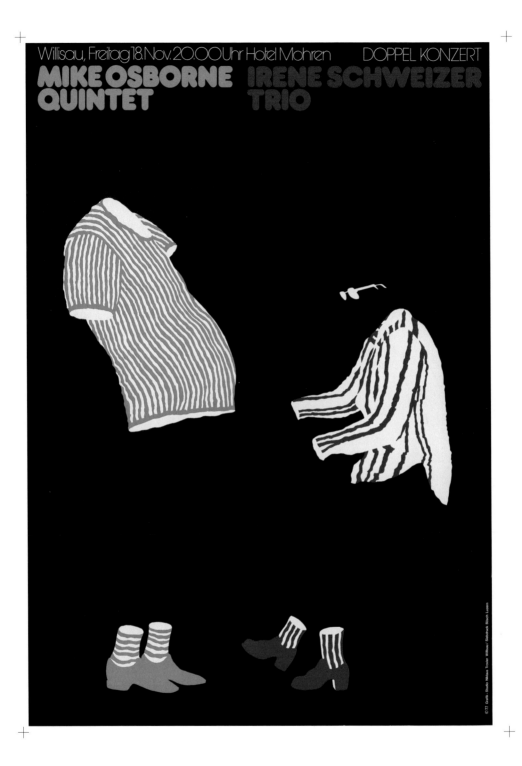

28 **Mike Osborne Quintet / Irène Schweizer Trio**
1977

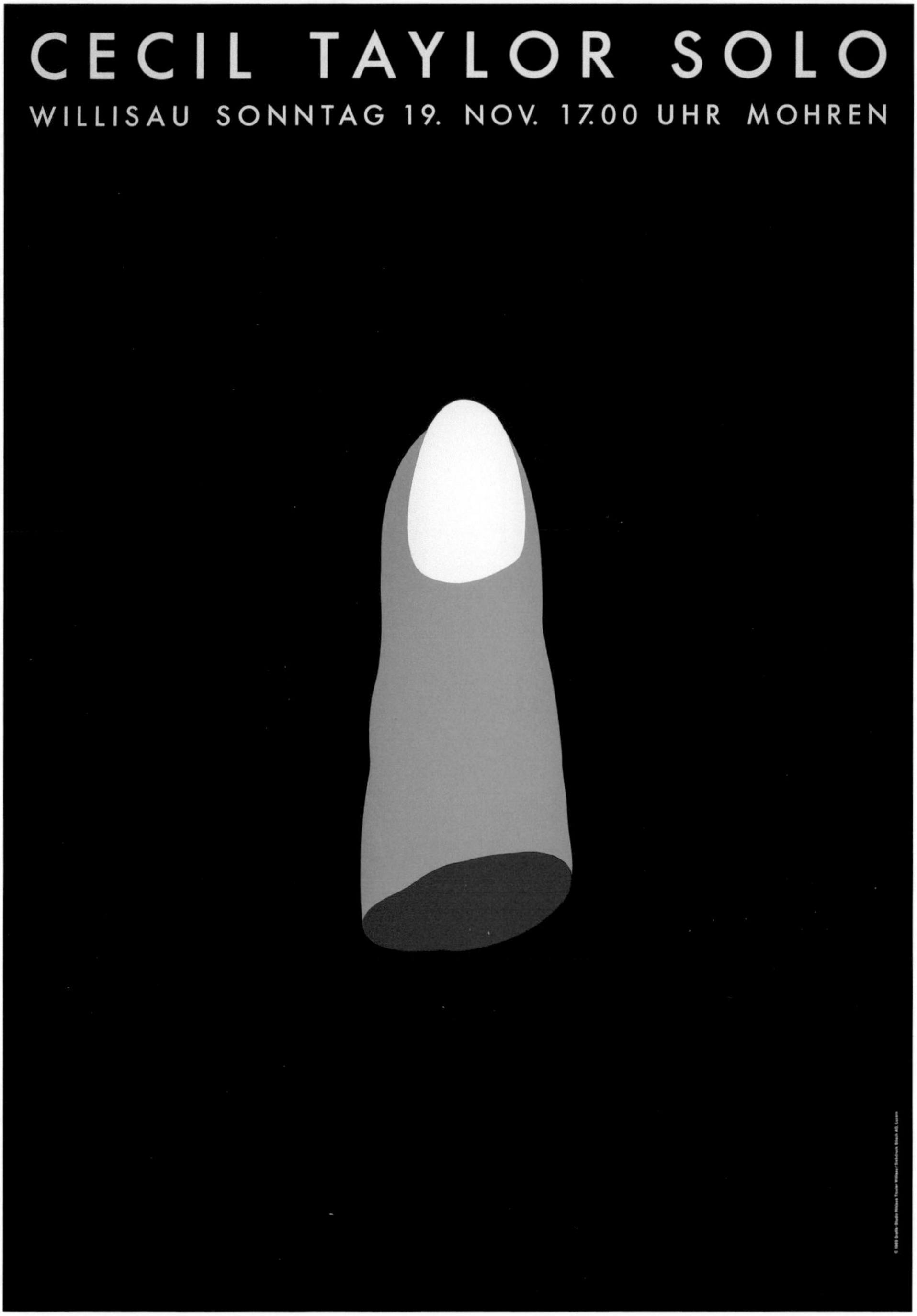

CECIL TAYLOR SOLO

WILLISAU SONNTAG 19. NOV. 17.00 UHR MOHREN

29 **Cecil Taylor Solo**
1989

30 **Niklaus Troxler / Jazz'n'more / Plakate**
2017

31 **American Indian Jazz & Dance /
Jim Pepper's Pow Wow**
1985

32 **Tim Berne's Paraphrase**
1998

33 **Brasil Jazz Night / Hermeto Pascoal e Grupo**
1985

34 **African Echoes / Abdullah Ibrahim Dollar Brand /
Pat Hall Smith – Warren Smith**
1988

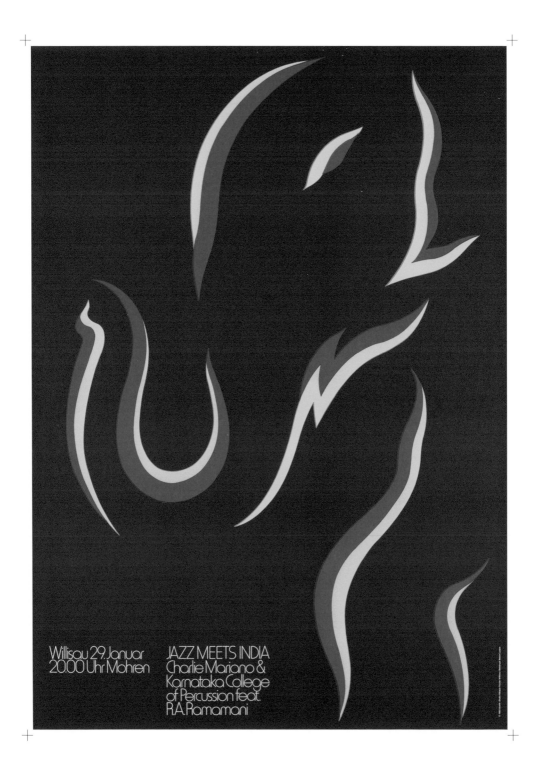

Willisau 29. Januar 20.00 Uhr Mohren JAZZ MEETS INDIA Charlie Mariano & Karnataka College of Percussion feat. R.A. Ramamani

35 **Jazz Meets India / Charlie Mariano &**
Karnataka College of Percussion Feat.
R.A. Ramamani
1983

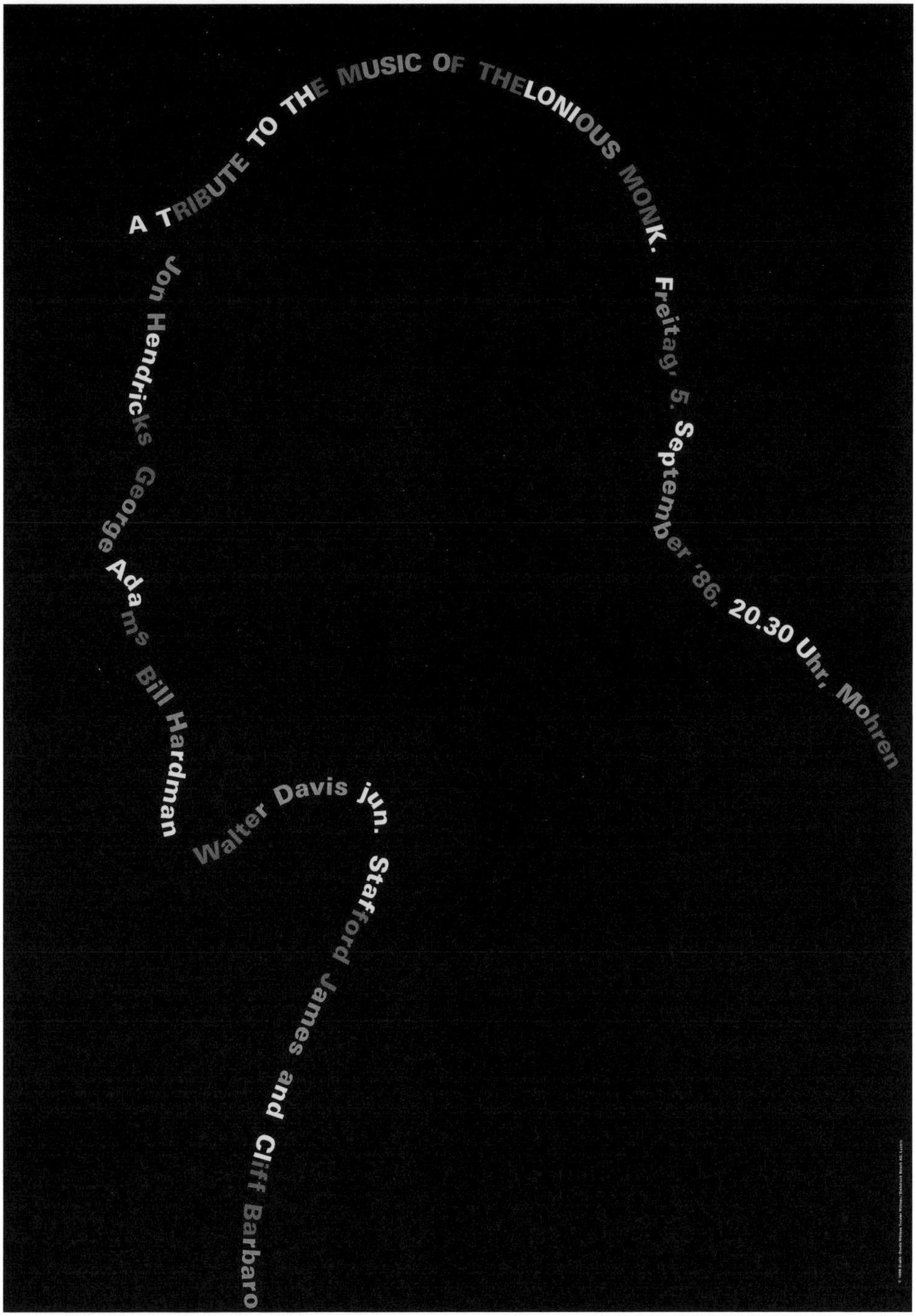
A TRIBUTE TO THE MUSIC OF THELONIOUS MONK.
Freitag, 5. September '86, 20.30 Uhr, Mohren
Jon Hendricks George Adams Bill Hardman Walter Davis jun. Stafford James and Cliff Barbaro

36 **A Tribute to the Music of Thelonious Monk.**
1986

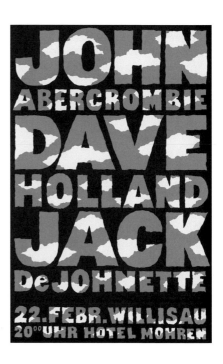

37 **20 Jahre Kleintheater Luzern**
1987

38 **Schluss mit der Schwarzmalerei!**
2010

39 **Tania Maria**
1988

40 **John Abercrombie /**
Dave Holland / Jack DeJohnette
1975

41 **Willem Breuker Kollektief**
1990

JAZZ FOR THE EYE:
ON THE AESTHETICS OF NIKLAUS TROXLER'S POSTER DESIGN

Daniel Martin Feige

In jazz music, the terms "ahead" and "laid back" refer to playing styles that are slightly ahead of or behind the beat. They are part of how jazz develops its idiosyncratic rhythmic drive and why it is a musical form whose entire success is at stake with every phrase. Time and timing must not be lost in the process, because otherwise the corresponding playing around and playing on the beat lose their meaning. In a modified way, this dictum even applies to the open forms of free jazz, in which the musicians' individual turns also may or may not fit.

I begin this essay with a remark on the rhythmic nature of jazz because jazz has shaped Niklaus Troxler's work like no other art form. Just as importantly, jazz is not just something that can be "on spot" or slightly off. It is a musical form that can capture or miss a certain era and attitude toward life. The same applies to posters, and especially to Troxler's posters: they get to the heart of their themes and their time in a condensed way.

A VISUAL HISTORY OF JAZZ

Troxler's jazz posters for the Willisau Jazz Festival, which he founded in 1975 and whose role in the spread, and indirectly the development, of jazz in Europe cannot be underestimated, have become a key component of the visual history of jazz. The graphic dimension may be less pronounced in jazz than in pop, which, as Diedrich Diederichsen has convincingly shown,[1] is not exclusively music, but is a complex combination of music, covers, fashion, poses, and so on. But graphic and pictorial aspects are by no means irrelevant to jazz, either. In addition to Francis Wolff's iconic photographs for Blue Note, Troxler's posters must also be mentioned in a European context since they have given jazz a specific face.

The proximity to jazz goes beyond the fact that this music is the motive and subject of many of Troxler's works. In the following, I would like to attempt to read his posters themselves as an expression of a musical logic. After all, poster art (as is in fact the case with all the arts, despite purist declarations to the contrary) is an aesthetic form that is informed in many ways by other arts and must therefore be considered in an intermedial context of various aesthetic media. The central idea I develop with regard to some of the posters shown here is this: it is not a contingent fact or simply a piece of biographical information that Troxler designed many posters devoted to jazz. Rather, his graphic language has a great affinity with this music. This means that the connection between jazz and graphic design, which I choose here as an approach, can be key to understanding his work. Troxler's posters are jazz for the eye.

1 See Diedrich Diederichsen, "Introduction," in: *Über Pop-Musik,* Cologne 2014.

THE POSTER AS A DISCIPLINE OF GRAPHIC DESIGN

Design and jazz have an important commonality, especially in a conventional understanding of the arts: they are quasi-illegitimate, borderline art forms. Until a few decades ago, it was commonly written that jazz was aesthetically impoverished compared to European art music[2] because, due to its improvisational character, it could not achieve the complexity of orchestral compositions from Viennese Classicism to Late Romanticism. And the poster, for its part, has often been excluded from art discourse because of its obvious functional character compared to paradigmatic painted works. Such theses are problematic because they apply inappropriate criteria to the respective objects. At the same time, the question arises: does not the poster belong in the realm of design rather than that of the arts? Despite the many ways in which the lines between the two spheres are blurred today, the distinction between art and design is important and should not be hastily abandoned. A poster informing a potential audience about an upcoming concert is not the same as a painting that aims to be viewed for the sake of the experience itself. Even if a poster can be looked at with the same attitude as an abstract painting, that does not make it one.

The distinction between art and design is in any case only problematic if it is understood to be a judgment in the sense of a hierarchical distinction.[3] The concept of applied art has often been explained in such a way that the applied arts qua applied are aesthetically less relevant or valuable than the liberal arts. This is a fallacy.[4] The poster as a discipline of graphic design can thus be understood as a field of aesthetic objects and as a specific aesthetic form that, even if it is not counted among the fine arts, is influenced by their aspects in many ways and is by no means subordinate to them in terms of relevance and value. The poster is an aesthetic practice of its own—and it is here that graphic design demonstrates very clearly how the history of the visual arts has also informed functional objects.

THE MUSICALITY OF POSTERS

Against this backdrop, in what way can we concretely describe the specific proximity of the graphic language of Troxler's posters to jazz? It is certainly not to be understood as exemplifying the element of intoxication that is sometimes (and often wrongly) attributed to jazz. In European jazz, for example, one might think of Peter Brötzmann's *Machine Gun,* or in American jazz, of John Coltrane's late albums with their religiousness exaggerated into the mystical. Troxler's visual language is more subdued and restrained in comparison to such descriptions, and its relationship to jazz will be shown below paradigmatically by means of interpretive remarks on some of his posters.

Let us start with a look at a real classic: the poster for the McCoy Tyner Sextet concert from 1980 1. The interplay between the yellow foreground and violet background and the accompanying visual contrast represent a graphically striking approach that fully explores the typography in its spatial and pictorial dimension–which is ultimately a

2 Paradigmatic here is the remark by Denis Dutton reported on by Philip Alperson in his canonical text on musical improvisation, see Philip Alperson, "On Musical Improvisation," in: *The Journal of Aesthetics and Art Criticism* 43 (1984), pp. 17–29, here p. 22.
3 For the systematic development of these considerations, see also Daniel Martin Feige, *Design: Eine philosophische Analyse,* Berlin 2018, esp. chapter 4.

signum of all graphic design that works with typography. The poster also expresses movement; the contrasting letters merge without losing their contours. If posters are understood not merely as a formal play of signs, but in such a way that they thematize concrete content in their aesthetic design, one could go further and say: the dynamics of foreground and background, of legibility and illegibility (occurring when the letters dissolve into the colors), are a graphic interpretation of the dynamics of McCoy Tyner's way of playing, which unfolds less in terms of conventional arcs of tension dictated by harmonies and more in terms of scales that do not themselves already entail certain tensions and relaxations. The same applies to the interaction of the musicians involved, which characteristically also functions according to a logic in which the musicians gradually move into the foreground and background (think, for example, of the accompaniment of a musician playing a solo). Seen in this light, this poster is not merely a graphic object that is already virtuosic in itself, but a work that actually articulates something about the specific dynamics of its subject through the form of its design.

In the poster promoting the concert by John Abercrombie, Dave Holland, and Jack DeJohnette, which Troxler created for the premiere year of the Willisau Jazz Festival, the central focus is also on typography 40. Unlike the previous example, however, this poster works with the contrast of light blue typography and dark blue background, the typography being interspersed with white areas that, read representationally, appear as clouds. Again, there is an interplay between foreground and background, but the poster is designed to be "seen through." The typography is used metonymically: not only does it point to a future musical event, but it also provides a glimpse into the sky, into the open, which was characteristic of the three musicians' playing in the 1970s. Due to the blurred letters, which do not have uniform edges but small irregularities on all sides, the poster develops a peculiar dynamic and appears almost kinetic despite its static layout.

At first glance, Troxler chose a completely different approach for the poster he created for David Murray's solo concert 59 twenty-six years later. It is based on a clear structure that at first seems quite simple: smaller and larger yellow and pink dots connected by straight lines, with the letters set in the larger circles. The real theme of the poster, however, is the tension between this clear, almost mechanical composition and Murray's energetic way of playing. In the sense of a change of aspect, it can be read as representational, on the one hand, and as an abstract composition, on the other. As such, its simple structure not only evokes associations with mathematics, physics, and, not least, electricity; the aforementioned tension also gives it a dynamic character, almost making it vibrate before the eyes. The poster created in 1991 for the 700th anniversary of the founding of Switzerland 95 shows in exemplary fashion that the affinity to jazz applies not only to those posters that explicitly have jazz as their subject: the correspondence and difference of the four drawn lines operate with identifiable elements, but as a poster it also develops a mobile and improvisational character.

4 Ironically, when design is proclaimed the new leading aesthetic discipline, the same mistake is repeated but with reversed roles, as can be seen by more recent developments in social design, critical design, and speculative design, including the participating discourses in design research, design thinking, and other design fields.

METONYMY AND METAPHOR, WIT AND VIRTUOSITY

Further interpretive perspectives open up with regard to posters which are pictorial in a representationalist way. Here "representation" simply means that images can be representations of something. Not all images exemplify colors and shapes; many show objects, persons, or situations. Such a semantic dimension cannot be considered independently of the way a poster is designed, insofar as posters (and this connects them to paintings as much as to novels) only thematize something by the way they thematize it. The American philosopher of art Arthur C. Danto has aptly pointed out here that the form of representation itself must be understood as an aspect of content;[5] one cannot, so to speak, see through the objects to what they show, but must pay attention to the specific way in which they are shown. In Troxler's posters, this meaningful dimension in the sensuality of forms, colors, and surfaces is not always and consistently played out in accordance with the formal play of typographic and spatial idiosyncrasies that has just been identified interpretively. Many posters are certainly representational in nature.

For example, the 1978 poster for the concert by the Anthony Braxton Quartet 15, a key representative of the Third Stream genre, which softened the lines between jazz and new music, shows an enigmatic landscape with scattered oversized parts of an instrument (or are there several?) and a person playing an equally oversized saxophone. The poster can be read as the graphic equivalent of Braxton's thoroughly idiosyncratic soundscapes. Don Pullen, on the other hand, is shown playing a piano 12 whose symmetrically placed keys become part of the Stars and Stripes flag. One cannot help but ascribe a political grammar to the poster as well, as the American flag emerges spatially from the playing of a musician who is a person of color.

Many of these more representational posters also have an enigmatic quality. Whereas the poster announcing a solo concert by Dave Holland 10 presents a bass synecdochically as a person, the iconic poster for Cecil Taylor's solo concert in 1989 is indecipherable in a productive way 29. Its severed green finger, set against a black background, is an object that, in the context of the formation of psychoanalytic theory, lies both within and outside the economy of understanding. But Troxler's posters also contain a great deal of visual wit—for example, when the saxophone is used as a telephone in the poster for George Coleman's concert 11, or when, in another poster, the same instrument is transformed into a snake 18, expressing to a certain extent the bite of jazz.

THE PERFORMATIVE DIMENSION OF POSTER ART

Not only do Niklaus Troxler's posters have a visual energy of their own, but they often demonstrate visual wit and virtuosity. Reading them in context and in tension with jazz illustrates that this energy, wit, and virtuosity have much in common with successful jazz improvisations. It is no coincidence that Troxler has recently created murals ("Tape Works") with colored and black adhesive tapes in his live performances accom-

---

5 See Arthur C. Danto, *The Transfiguration of the Commonplace: A Philosophy of Art,* Cambridge, MA 1981, esp. chapter 6.

panied by jazz musicians. One example is the poster "Tape & Jazz" 104, which itself works with such adhesive tapes and thus gives rise to typographic as well as pictorial and abstract forms. This practice represents a consistent radicalization of the sensibilities already evident in his early posters. In his representational images and works that spatialize typography, Troxler approaches the unsecured, open, and improvisational character of jazz like hardly any other graphic designer.

BOB STEWART GROUP Willisau, 16. Mai 87, 20 Uhr, Mohren

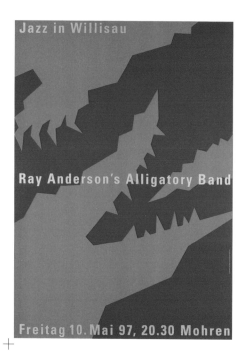

42 **Bob Stewart Group**
1987

43 **Ray Anderson's Alligatory Band**
1997

44 **Bob Stewart Tuba / Arthur Blythe Alto Sax**
2005

45 **SGV Generalversammlung**
1989

Kurtheater Baden Sonntag 22. Nov. 87, 19.00 Uhr

TRIBUTE TO FATS WALLER

Ralph Sutton, Jim Galloway, Milt Hinton, Gus Johnson
Henri Chaix, Alain Du Bois, Romano Cavicchiolo
Vorverkauf: SKA, Badstrasse 8, Baden. Tel. 056-20 12 01

46 **Tribute to Fats Waller**
1987

47 **Olma St. Gallen**
1994

48 **Elsi, die seltsame Magd**
1994

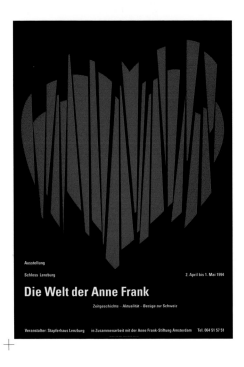

49 **Die Spielverderber**
1994

50 **Die Welt der Anne Frank**
1994

51 **Otello**
1991

52 **Keramik-Ausstellung**
1994

Das Lachen

nach dem gleichnamigen Essay

des französischen Philosophen Henri Bergson

Eine internationale Produktion des

MAD Theaters mit

Komikern und Komikerinnen

aus sechs Ländern

Premiere 3. und 4. Sept. 93

20.30 Uhr

im ehemaligen Schlachthaus

Zofingen

Unterstützt von Pro Helvetia,

Stadt Bern, Stadt Zofingen

53 **Das Lachen**
1993

54 **Knie**
1981

0. April – 28. Mai

Jazz in Willisau
In. Okt. 75 20.00 h
Ni 220
CH-6130 Hotel Mohren
Switzerland

U.S.Postage 10c

2öc AIRMAIL
Shrine of Democracy
USA
1249'5

EXPRÈS
Special Delivery
POD Label 57
GPO 16-74142-1

BY AIR MAIL
PAR AVION

Joe McPhee
Trio
Porshheepcie
N.Y. 12601 USA

55 **Joe McPhee Trio**
1975

56 **Keith Jarrett Quartet**
1976

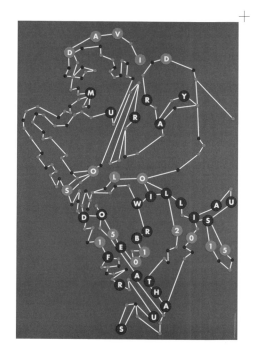

57 **Stu Martin**
1973

58 **Uli Kempendorff & Friends**
2014

59 **David Murray Solo**
2001

60 **The Trio / John Surman /
Barre Phillips / Stu Martin**
1976

61 **Arthur Blythe Quartet**
1982

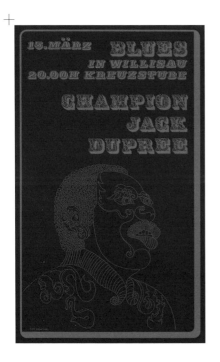

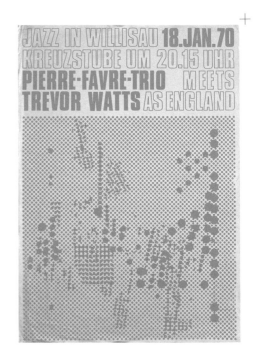

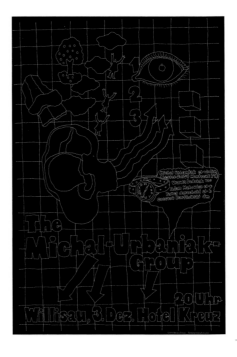

62 **Blues in Willisau / Champion Jack Dupree**
1970

63 **Kenny Wheeler Quartet**
2001

64 **Pierre-Favre-Trio Meets Trevor Watts**
1970

65 **The Michal-Urbaniak-Group**
1971

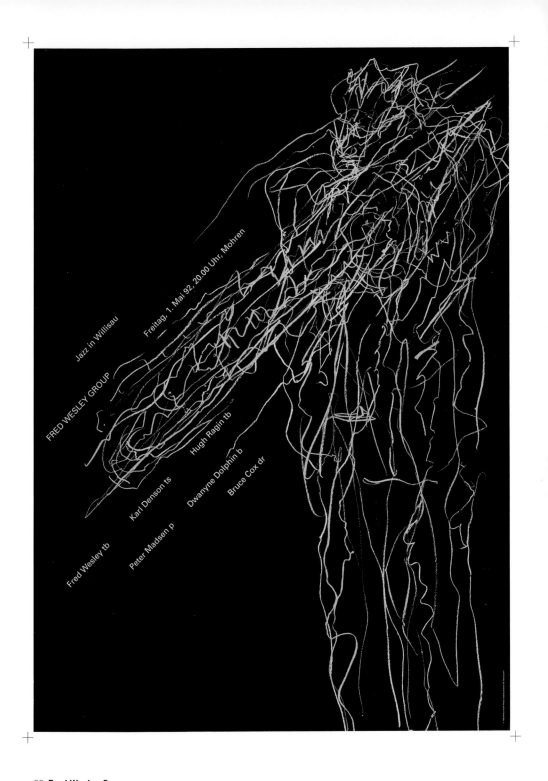

Jazz in Willisau   Freitag, 1. Mai 92, 20.00 Uhr, Mohren

FRED WESLEY GROUP

Hugh Ragin tb

Karl Denson ts   Dwanyne Dolphin b   Bruce Cox dr

Fred Wesley tb   Peter Madsen p

66 **Fred Wesley Group**
1992

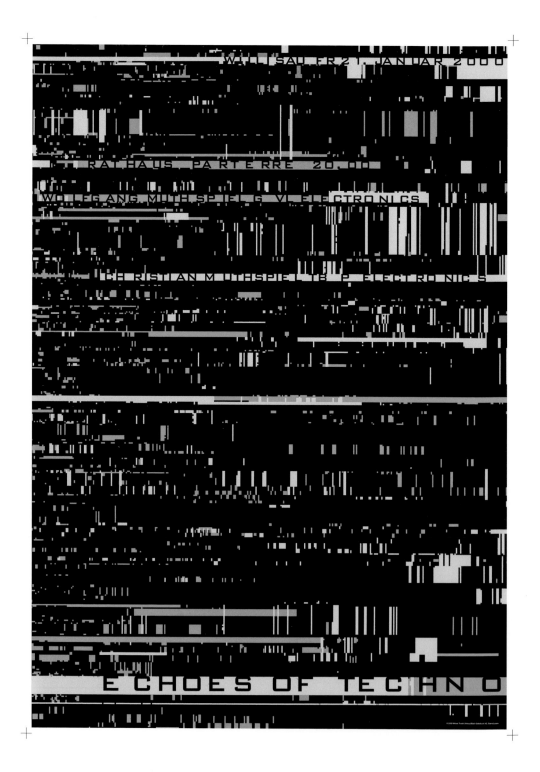

67 **Echoes of Techno**
2000

68 **OM / Christy Doran / Bobby Burri /
Urs Leimgruber / Fredy Studer**
2016

69 **The Workers**
2019

70 **Maria João Vocal / Aki Takase Piano**
1988

71 **Luca Sisera / Roofer**
2020

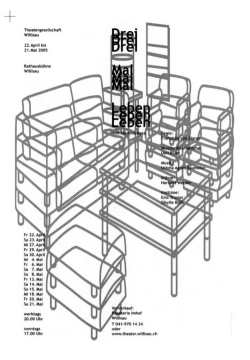

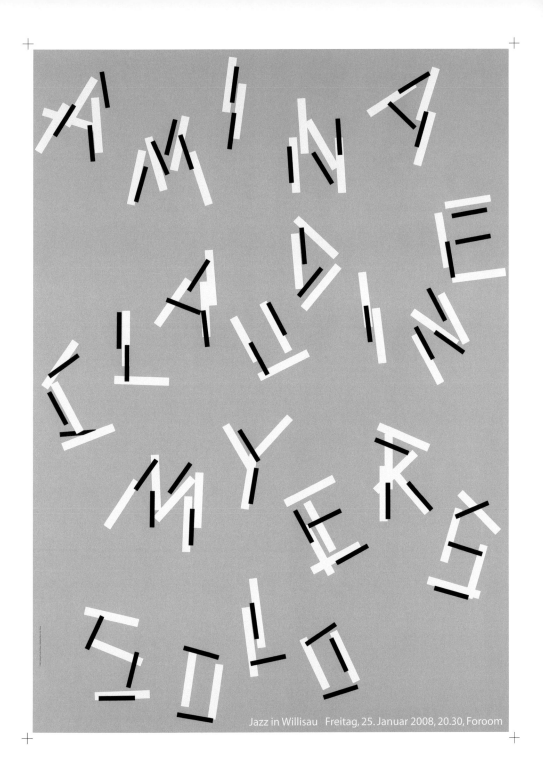

76 **Amina Claudine Myers Solo**
2008

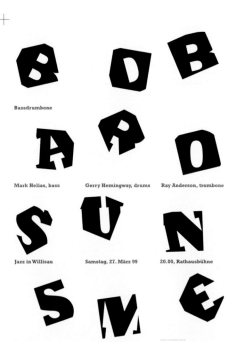

Bassdrumbone

Mark Helias, bass   Gerry Hemingway, drums   Ray Anderson, trombone

Jazz in Willisau   Samstag, 27. März 99   20.00, Rathausbühne

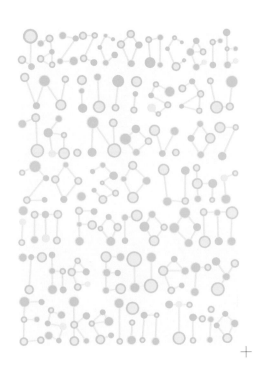

77 **BassDrumBone / Mark Helias /
Gerry Hemingway / Ray Anderson**
1999

78 **Christy Doran's New Bag**
2002

79 **Charles Gayle Solo**
2009

80 **The Ellery Eskelin Trio**
2007

81 **Simon Nabatov / Piano Solo**
2003

Typo Plakate

Ausstellung
im Rathaus
Willisau

18. bis 27. Mai 1996

Eugen Bachmann
Sandra Binder
Georges Calame
Peter Erni
Roli Fischbacher
K. D. Geissbühler
Armin Hofmann
Melchior Imboden
Werner Jeker
Theo Leuthold
Hans-Rudolf Lutz
Bruno Monguzzi
Andrea Muheim
Lars Müller
Pierre Neumann
Siegfried Odermatt
Roger Pfund
Marc Philipp
Daniela Schmid
Peter Scholl
Ralph Schraivogel
George Staehelin
Tino Steinemann
Rosmarie Tissi
Simone Torelli
Niklaus Troxler
Martine Waltzer
Wolfgang Weingart
Ruedi Wyss
Dario Zuffo

Öffnungszeiten:
So 15.5. 10-12   14-17
Fr 24.5.   19-21
Sa 25.5. 10-12   14-17
So 26.5. 10-12   14-17
Mo 27.5. 10-12   14-17

82 **Typo Plakate**
1996

If you cover Helvetica it looks quite nice

HELVETICA 50 YEARS. Designed by NIKLAUS TROXLER, Willisau
on the occasion of the celebration of «Helvetica, 50 Years» and the European Premiere of «Helvetica, A Documentary Film by Gary Hustwit» in Zürich, on March 24, 2007.
An initiative by Lars Müller in collaboration with the Museum of Design Zürich, sponsored by the Swiss Federal Office of Culture.

83 **If You Cover Helvetica It Looks Quite Nice**
2007

Eine offene Schweiz, s.v.p.!

84 **Eine offene Schweiz, s.v.p.!**
2016

BLUTENDE BÄUME, TRUNKENE FLAGGEN
Bettina Richter

Niklaus Troxler glaubt an die Wirkungsmacht des Plakats. Dabei vertraut er nicht nur auf die gestalterische Verführungskraft seiner Kulturplakate, als engagierter Zeitgenosse greift er mit seinen politischen Plakaten pointiert in Gegenwartsdiskurse ein und bezieht Position.

Bereits ein Klassiker der Plakatgeschichte ist Troxlers Plakat «Tote Bäume» von 1992 7, das ursprünglich auf Einladung der UN-Konferenz für Umwelt und Entwicklung in Rio de Janeiro entstand, jedoch als zu gewalttätig abgelehnt wurde. Mit Unterstützung der Allgemeinen Plakatgesellschaft Schweiz konnte Troxler das Plakat dennoch drucken und in der Schweiz aushängen. Es funktioniert ganz ohne Worte und ist damit universal und zeitlos verständlich. Der harte Komplementärkontrast Rot-Grün, die sich scheinbar unendlich fortsetzende Reihung der Baumstümpfe und ihre Schnittflächen, die an blutige Wunden erinnern, erscheinen im Rückblick als traurige Prophezeiung internationaler Tatenlosigkeit.[1]

Plakativ im besten Sinne des Wortes und ein Plädoyer für mehr Zivilcourage ist das Textplakat «Gewalt! Halt!» 86, in dem sich die serifenlosen Grossbuchstaben «W» und «H» überlagern. Mit ebenso massiven Majuskeln arbeitet Troxler im Plakat «Steuerflu[ch]t» 89, hier mit der Auslassung der sinngebenden Buchstabenfolge «CH». Die Botschaften und deren visuelle Vermittlung mögen vereinfachend sein, eine Störung im konsumorientierten Umfeld bedeuten sie auf alle Fälle. Ein Plakat erfüllt seinen Zweck, wenn es sich im hektischen Stadtgetriebe blitzschnell Aufmerksamkeit verschaffen und im Bildgedächtnis verankern kann. Komplexe Tiefe widerspricht seinen medialen Gesetzen. Diese Erfahrung nutzt Troxler, um mit markanten Wortspielen oder mit symbolträchtigen, emotional besetzten Bildern Aufsehen zu erregen.

Zu diesen Bildern zählt auch die Nationalflagge. Als 1995 die Initiative für einen Beitrag der Schweiz zur Europäischen Union lanciert wurde, gestaltete Troxler im Eigenauftrag ein unmissverständliches Plakat 87: Das Schweizerkreuz in den Farben der EU verdeckt die rot-weisse Flagge. Auf die gemeinsam mit der Allgemeinen Plakatgesellschaft durchgeführte Hängung des Plakats in der Zentralschweiz gab es nach einer Woche so heftige Reaktionen, dass die Aktion schliesslich abgebrochen werden musste. Troxler folgte damit der Strategie des deutschen Politgrafikers Klaus Staeck, der sich die formalen Mechanismen der Werbung gezielt zunutze macht und das Irritationspotenzial seiner Plakate ebenfalls beträchtlich erhöht, indem er sie an offiziellen Aushangflächen plakatieren lässt.[2]

Gemeinsam mit Staeck, Jianping He und Yossi Lemel juriierte Troxler 2011 die Plakate des damals neu gegründeten internationalen Wettbewerbs «Mut zur Wut», der seither jährlich zur Gestaltung politischer Plakate einlädt und die prämierten öffentlich aushängt.[3] 2016 entwarf Troxler für diesen Wettbewerb das Plakat «Eine offene Schweiz, s.v.p.!» 84. Hier gerät das quadratische Mittelfeld des Schweizerkreuzes in Bewegung, die Bruchstellen werden zu einem Sinnbild offener Grenzen. Die Abkürzung «s.v.p.» für das französische «s'il vous plaît» ist gleichzeitig Kürzel der rechtskonservativen Schweizerischen Volkspartei, die für ihre fremdenfeindliche Politik bekannt ist.

Nochmals dominiert 2021 eine Flagge – oder vielmehr ihre unverkennbaren Bildelemente – ein Plakat mit dem wortspielerischen Titel «Demo Crazy» 88. Troxler lud hier ein 1994 entstandenes Konzertplakat mit neuer Bedeutung auf. Sterne und Streifen der US-Flagge lösen sich aus ihrer festgelegten Ordnung, taumeln trunken umher und erinnern an den Sturm wütender Trump-Anhänger auf das Kapitol in Washington nach dessen Wahlniederlage. Das angerichtete Chaos wurde weltweit als Angriff auf die Demokratie verurteilt.

Im selben Jahr gestaltete Troxler ein Plakat mit den sprichwörtlichen drei Affen 90, die er auf ihre piktogrammhaft abstrahierten Köpfe reduzierte. Das klassische «Nichts sehen, nichts hören, nichts sagen» wird in den Appell «Augen auf, Ohren auf, Mund auf» verkehrt. Der Aufruf zu mehr Engagement gewann gerade vor dem Hintergrund der weltweiten Pandemie an Bedeutung, als gelebte Solidarität im nächsten Umfeld ebenso wichtig wurde wie Wachsamkeit gegenüber Politik und Wirtschaft, die hinter den Kulissen nicht unbedeutende Entscheidungen fällten. Auch dieses Plakat hängte Troxler in Eigenregie in Willisau aus.

In seinen politischen Plakaten bedient sich Troxler meist einer anderen visuellen Sprache als in den Kulturplakaten. Flächige Gestaltung, formal verknappte Motive, leuchtende Farbigkeit und eindeutige Botschaften richten sich an ein grösstmögliches Publikum. Der japanische Gestalter Shigeo Fukuda äusserte sich folgendermassen über Troxlers Baum-Plakat: «Zu diesem Plakat braucht es keinen Kommentar. Es ist ein Requiem für die stumme Erde, welches nur Troxler allein komponieren konnte, weil er bis anhin stets den Ton visuell umgesetzt hat.»[4]

1 Verabschiedet wurde auf der Konferenz letztlich eine völkerrechtlich nicht bindende Waldgrundsatzerklärung.
2 Siehe dazu: Museum Folkwang (Hg.), *Sand fürs Getriebe. Plakate und Provokationen,* Göttingen 2018.
3 www.mutzurwut.com
4 Zit. nach: Niklaus Troxler (Hg.), *Jazz Blvd. Niklaus Troxler. Posters,* Baden 1999, S. 210.

BLEEDING TREES, DRUNKEN FLAGS
Bettina Richter

Niklaus Troxler believes in the power of the poster. And he does not simply rely on the seductive power of his cultural posters, but, as a socially engaged artist of his times, he also pointedly intervenes and takes a stand in contemporary discourse with his political posters.

Troxler's "Dead Trees" poster from 1992 7, which was originally created at the invitation of the UN Conference on Environment and Development in Rio de Janeiro, but rejected for being too violent, is a classic in poster history. With the support of the Swiss national advertising company Allgemeine Plakatgesellschaft Schweiz, Troxler was nevertheless able to print the poster and display

Niklaus und Ems Troxler beim Hängen des Plakats «Eine offene Schweiz, s.v.p.!» in Willisau, 2016 / Niklaus and Ems Troxler hanging the poster "An Open Switzerland, s.v.p.!" in Willisau, 2016. Photo: Norbert Bossart, Willisauer Bote

it in Switzerland. It operates entirely without words and is thus universally and timelessly comprehensible. In retrospect, the harsh complementary contrast of red and green, the seemingly endless series of tree stumps, and the cut surfaces reminiscent of bloody wounds appear as a sad prophecy of international inaction.[1]

The text poster "Gewalt! Halt!" (Violence! Stop!) 86, in which the sans serif capitals "W" and "H" overlap, is eye-catching and a plea for more civic courage. Troxler works with the same solid capital letters in the poster "Steuerflu[ch]t" (Tax Evasion) 89—in this case emphasizing the meaningful sequence of letters "CH," the abbreviation for Switzerland. The messages and the way they are visually conveyed may be simplistic, but they are definitely a disruption in a consumer-oriented environment. A poster fulfils its purpose if it can attract attention at lightning speed in the hustle and bustle of the city and anchor itself in visual memory. Complex depth contradicts the laws of the medium. Troxler uses this experience to cause a stir with striking wordplay or with symbolic, emotionally charged images.

These images also include the Swiss national flag. When the initiative for Switzerland's accession to the European Union was launched in 1995, Troxler took it upon himself to design a poster 87 that made a very clear statement: it shows the Swiss cross in the EU colors covering the red and white flag. Reactions to the poster being displayed in central Switzerland in colla-

boration with the Allgemeine Plakatgesellschaft were so intense within the first week that the campaign had to be cancelled. In the work, Troxler followed the strategy of German political graphic artist Klaus Staeck, who deliberately exploits the formal mechanisms of advertising and considerably increases the disruptive potential of his posters by displaying them on official billboards.[2]

In 2011, as part of a jury made up of Staeck, Jianping He, and Yossi Lemel, Troxler selected the winning posters for the newly founded international competition "Mut zur Wut" (Courage to Rage), which every year invites people to design political posters and publicly displays the award-winning ones.[3] In 2016 Troxler designed the poster "Eine offene Schweiz, s.v.p.!" (An Open Switzerland, s.v.p.!) 84 for this competition. Here, the square central field of the Swiss cross is set in motion, and the fractures become a symbol of open borders. The abbreviation "s.v.p." for the French "s'il vous plaît" is also the abbreviation of the right-wing conservative Schweizerische Volkspartei (Swiss People's Party), which is known for its xenophobic policies.

Once again in 2021, Troxler used a flag—or rather its unmistakable pictorial parts—as the dominant element in a poster with the pun-like title "Demo Crazy" 88. Here, he added new meaning to a concert poster he designed in 1994. The stars and stripes of the U.S. flag break free from their set configuration, stagger about drunkenly, and recall the storming of the Capitol in Washington, D.C., by angry Trump supporters after his election defeat. The chaos they wrought was condemned worldwide as an attack on democracy.

The same year Troxler designed a poster with the proverbial three monkeys 90, which he reduced to their pictogram-like abstracted heads. The classic "See nothing, hear nothing, say nothing" is inverted into the appeal "Augen auf, Ohren auf, Mund auf" (Eyes open, ears open, mouth open). This call for more engagement gained in importance against the backdrop of the worldwide pandemic, when lived solidarity in people's immediate surroundings became just as important as vigilance vis-à-vis politics and business, which were making significant decisions behind the scenes. Troxler also hung this poster in Willisau on his own initiative.

In his political posters, Troxler usually uses a different visual language than in his cultural ones. Two-dimensional design, formally concise motifs, bright colors, and unambiguous messages are aimed at the largest possible audience. The Japanese designer Shigeo Fukuda had this to say about Troxler's tree poster: "With such a poster, commentary is superfluous. It is a requiem for our silent, gagged planet, a work which only Troxler could have created, as the great master of visualizing sound."[4]

1 The conference ultimately adopted a declaration of forest principles that is not binding under international law.
2 See also Museum Folkwang (ed.), *Sand fürs Getriebe: Plakate und Provokationen,* Göttingen 2018.
3 www.mutzurwut.com
4 Cited in Niklaus Troxler (ed.), *Jazz Blvd.: Niklaus Troxler, Posters,* Baden 1999, p. 210.

85 **Hilfe für das sexuell ausgebeutete Kind**
1997

86 **Gewalt! Halt!**
1993

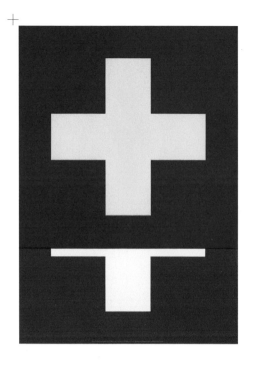

87 **[CH – EU]**
1996

88 **Demo Crazy**
2021

89 **Steuerflu[ch]t**
2013

90 **Augen auf / Ohren auf / Mund auf**
2021

91 **WWF / For a Living Planet**
2005

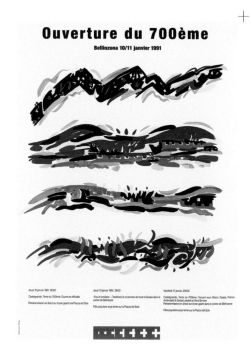

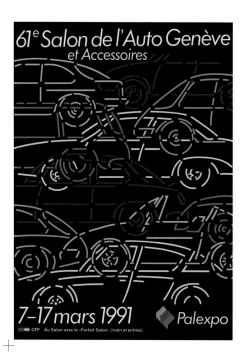

92 **Schlussfeier in Basel /**
700 Jahre Eidgenossenschaft
1991

93 **61ᵉ Salon de l'Auto et**
Accessoires Genève
1991

94 **Ouverture du 700ᵉᵐᵉ**
1991

95 **Fest der vier Kulturen / Utopien /**
700 Jahre Eidgenossenschaft
1991

Jetzt mit farbigem TV-Magazin

97 **Vaterland / Die Zeitung mit Linie**
1991

98 **Vaterland / Die Zeitung mit Linie**
1989

99 **Vaterland / Die Zeitung mit Linie**
1989

100 **Vaterland / Die Zeitung mit Linie**
1989

101 **Sörenberg-Flühli**
2015

102 **Gianluigi Trovesi / Gianni Coscia Duo**
1999

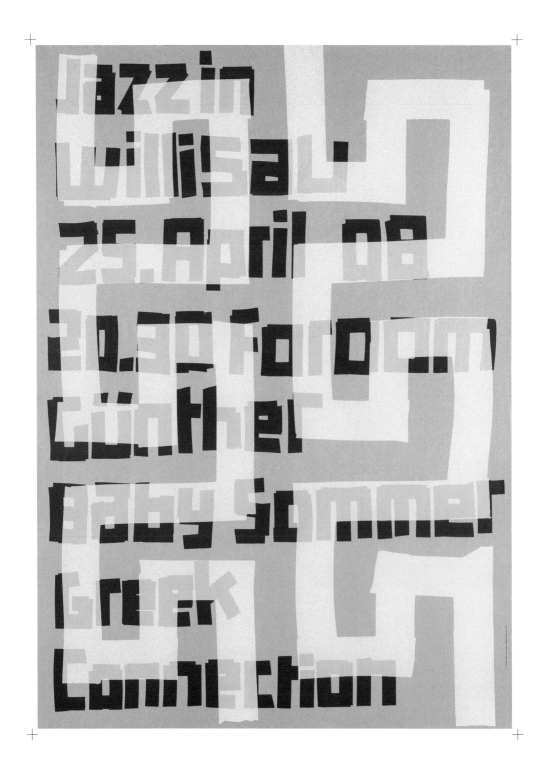

103 **Baby Sommer / Greek Connection**
2008

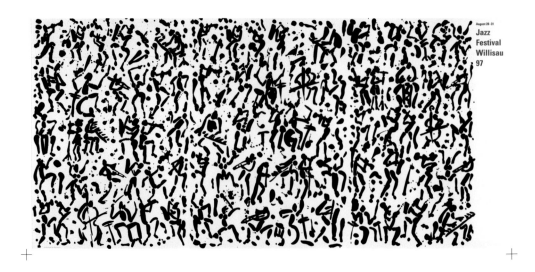

105 **Jazz Festival Willisau '08**
2008

106 **Jazz Festival Willisau 97**
1997

Samstag 27. Februar 2016, 20.00 Uhr, Jazz im bau 4, Altbüron

Tree Ear. Sebastian Stinning ts, Gerry Hemingway dr, Manuel Troller g

107 **Tree Ear. Sebastian Stinning,
Gerry Hemingway, Manuel Troller**
2016

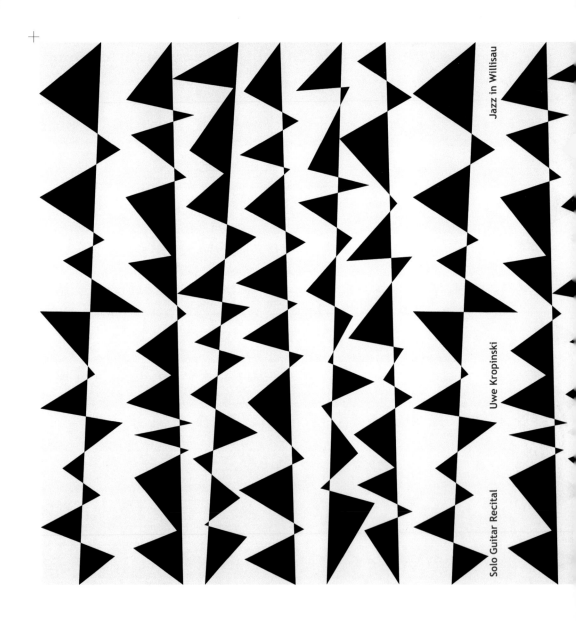

Jazz in Willisau

Uwe Kropinski

Solo Guitar Recital

108 **Solo Guitar Recital / Uwe Kropinski**
1998

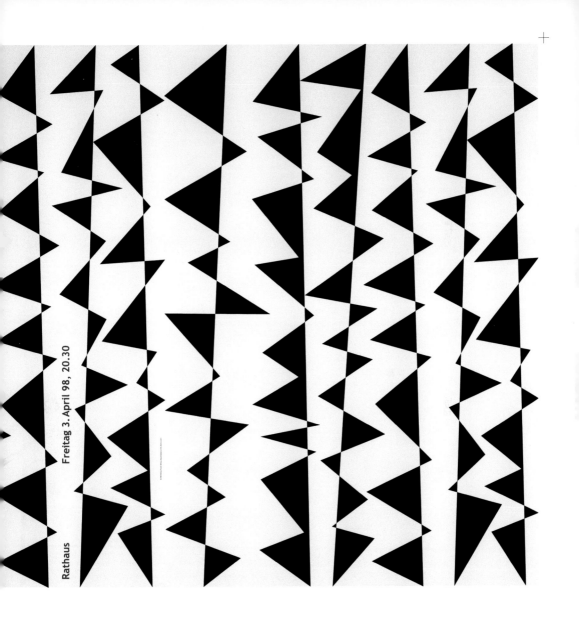

Rathaus Freitag 3. April 98, 20.30

Niklaus Troxler

Geboren am 1. Mai 1947 in Willisau.

Niklaus Troxler absolvierte von 1963 bis 1967 zunächst
eine Lehre als Schriftsetzer und besuchte parallel dazu
Kurse an der Schule für Gestaltung in Luzern, wo er
sich von 1967 bis 1971 zum Grafiker ausbilden liess. 1972
arbeitete Troxler als Art Director in Paris bei Hollenstein
Création. Zurück in der Schweiz, gründete er 1973
ein eigenes Grafikstudio in Willisau. Von 1966 bis 2013
organisierte Troxler Konzerte in Willisau («Jazz in Willisau»),
ab 1975 zudem ein jährliches Jazzfestival, dessen Leitung
er 2010 an seinen Neffen Arno Troxler übergab. Von
1998 bis 2013 unterrichtete Troxler als Professor für
Kommunikationsdesign und Illustration an der Staatlichen
Akademie der Bildenden Künste in Stuttgart. Zudem hielt
er weltweit regelmässig Vorträge und leitete Workshops.

1982 wurde Troxler der Innerschweizer Kulturpreis
zuerkannt, 1984 erhielt er das Eidgenössische Stipendium
für angewandte Kunst. Seine Plakate wurden wiederholt
beim Wettbewerb «Schweizer Plakate des Jahres»
unter dem Patronat des Eidgenössischen Departements
des Innern (EDI) und vom Art Directors Club Schweiz
(ADC Schweiz) ausgezeichnet. Troxler erhielt auch
zahlreiche internationale Preise für sein Plakatschaffen.
Seine Arbeiten fanden sich häufig unter den «100 Besten
Plakaten Deutschland-Österreich-Schweiz». 1987 und
erneut 1994 wurde ihm die Henri-de-Toulouse-Lautrec-
Goldmedaille der Stadt Essen verliehen. Der Tokyo
Type Directors Club ebenso wie der Type Directors Club
New York würdigten sein Werk mit Auszeichnungen. Preise
und Ehrungen empfing er zudem bei den internationalen
Plakatbiennalen und -triennalen in Brünn, Chaumont,
Colorado, Hangzhou, Helsinki, Hongkong, Lahti, Ningbo,
Taipeh, Toyama, Trnava, Warschau und Zagreb.

Die Stadt Willisau ernannte Troxler 1994 zum Ehrenbürger.

Seit 1989 ist Troxler Mitglied der Alliance Graphique
Internationale. Seine Plakate sind in den wichtigsten
internationalen Designsammlungen vertreten. Sein Werk
wurde in zahlreichen nationalen und internationalen
Ausstellungen präsentiert.

Troxler ist mit der Willisauer Kunst- und Kulturschaffenden
Ems Troxler, geborene Bättig, verheiratet und Vater der
drei Töchter Kathrin, Annik und Paula. Er lebt und arbeitet
heute in Willisau und Berlin.

Niklaus Troxler

Born in Willisau on May 1, 1947.

Niklaus Troxler did an apprenticeship as a typesetter
from 1963 to 1967 and at the same time attended
courses at the Lucerne School of Design, where he
trained as a graphic designer from 1967 to 1971. In 1972
he worked as an art director for Hollenstein Création
in Paris. Back in Switzerland, he founded his own
graphic design studio in Willisau in 1973. From 1966
to 2013, he organized concerts in Willisau ("Jazz in
Willisau"), and from 1975, an annual jazz festival, the
direction of which he handed over to his nephew
Arno Troxler in 2010. From 1998 to 2013, Troxler served
as a professor of communication design and illustration
at the Stuttgart State Academy of Art and Design.
Furthermore, he regularly gave lectures and led workshops around the world.

In 1982 Troxler was awarded the Cultural Prize of
Central Switzerland, and in 1984 he received the Swiss
Federal Scholarship for Applied Arts. His posters have
won numerous awards in the "Swiss Poster of the Year"
competition of the Swiss Federal Department of Home
Affairs and have been honored on many occasions by
the Art Directors Club of Switzerland (ADC Switzerland).
Troxler has also received numerous international
prizes for his posters. His works have frequently been
listed among the "100 Best Posters of Germany, Austria,
and Switzerland." In 1987 and 1994 he was presented
with the Henri de Toulouse-Lautrec Gold Medal by the
city of Essen. His work has also garnered awards from
the Tokyo Type Directors Club and the Type Directors
Club of New York. Finally, he has received prizes and
honors at the international poster biennials and triennials
in Brno, Chaumont, Colorado, Hangzhou, Helsinki, Hong
Kong, Lahti, Ningbo, Taipei, Toyama, Trnava, Warsaw,
and Zagreb.

The town of Willisau made Troxler an honorary citizen
in 1994.

Troxler has been a member of the Alliance Graphique
Internationale since 1989. His posters are represented
in the most important international design collections,
and his work has been shown in numerous national and
international exhibitions.

Troxler is married to Ems Troxler, née Bättig, an artist
and cultural creator from Willisau. He is the father of
three daughters, Kathrin, Annik, and Paula. He currently
lives and works in Willisau and Berlin.

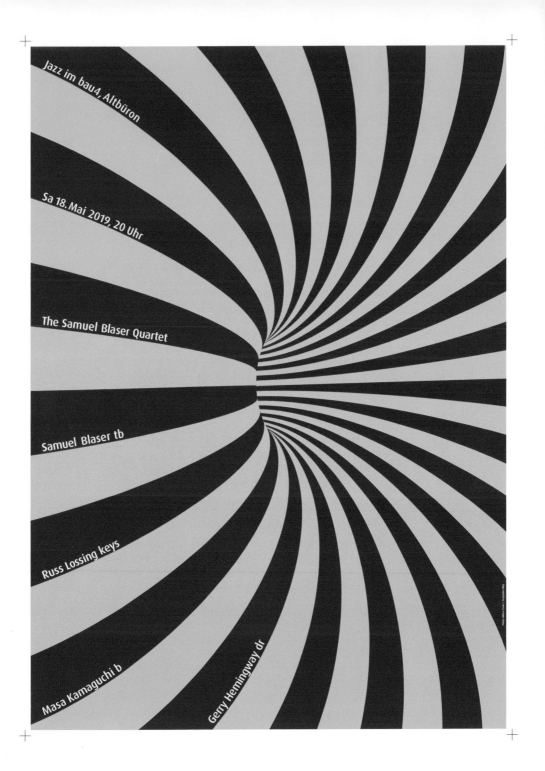

Jazz im bau4, Altbüron

Sa 18. Mai 2019, 20 Uhr

The Samuel Blaser Quartet

Samuel Blaser tb

Russ Lossing keys

Masa Kamaguchi b

Gerry Hemingway dr

109 **The Samuel Blaser Quartet**
2019

Katalog

Alle abgebildeten Plakate stammen aus der Plakat-sammlung des Museum für Gestaltung Zürich. Die Rechte (insbesondere Urheberrechte) liegen beim Autor. © 2022, ProLitteris, Zurich: Niklaus Troxler

Die Daten des Katalogs folgen den Rubriken Plakattext, Erscheinungsjahr, Erscheinungsland, Drucktechnik, Format. Dabei gelten insbesondere folgende Regelungen:

Plakattext: Die beste Textwiedergabe bildet die Abbildung des Plakates selbst. Darum wird hier eine vereinfachte Form wiedergegeben, welche nur die aussagekräftigen Textbestandteile berücksichtigt. Allfällige Umstellungen dienen der Verständlichkeit. Das Zeichen / trennt inhaltliche Texteinheiten. Jeweils in Klammern nachgestellt folgt die deutsche und/oder englische Übersetzung.

Erscheinungsland: Das Erscheinungsland wird mit dem international gebräuchlichen ISO-Code angegeben. Da die meisten Plakate von Niklaus Troxler in der Schweiz im Aushang waren, wird in der vorliegenden Publikation das Erscheinungsland nur dann genannt, wenn davon abweichend.

Format: Die Angaben werden in der Abfolge Höhe × Breite und in cm gemacht. Weil die Plakate oft nicht exakt rechtwinklig geschnitten sind, werden die Abmessungen auf halbe cm aufgerundet.

Donationsnachweis: Alle Plakate in der vorliegenden Publikation sind als Donation von Niklaus Troxler in die Plakatsammlung gelangt.

Die Plakatgeschichte ist ein junges Forschungsgebiet – verlässliche Hinweise sind rar. Jeder Hinweis und jede Ergänzung sind willkommen: sammlungen@museum-gestaltung.ch

Catalogue

All posters reproduced are from the Museum für Gestaltung Zürich's Poster Collection. The copyrights are held by the author. © 2022, ProLitteris, Zurich: Niklaus Troxler

The data listed in the catalogue is broken down into the following sections: poster title and/or text, year and country of first appearance, printing technique, size. In particular, the following rules have been applied:

Poster text: The poster itself provides the best version of the text, and thus a simplified form is used which provides only the most meaningful elements. Any rearrangements that have been made are for purposes of intelligibility. A slash mark separates textual units by content. The German and/or English translation is set in parentheses after the poster text.

Country of first appearance: The country of first appearance is identified by the internationally accepted ISO code. Since most of the posters by Niklaus Troxler first appeared in Switzerland, this publication only notes exceptions.

Format: The dimensions are given in centimeters as height × width. Because posters are often not cut exactly at right angles, the dimensions are rounded off to the half-centimeter.

Donor: All the posters in this publication were donated to the Poster Collection by Niklaus Troxler.

The history of posters is a recent field of research– reliable information is rare. Any further references or additional materials are welcome: sammlungen@museum-gestaltung.ch

1 Willisau Mohren / McCoy Tyner Sextet
1980 Siebdruck – Screen print
128 × 90,5 cm

2 Jazz im Bau 4 Altbüron / Ellery Eskelin / Christian Weber / Michael Griener
2019 Siebdruck – Screen print
128 × 90,5 cm

3 Jazz Festival Willisau 2000
2000 Siebdruck – Screen print
128 × 90,5 cm

4 Willisau Hotel Mohren / Anthony Cox Quartet Featuring Dewey Redman
1992 Siebdruck – Screen print
128 × 90,5 cm

5 Hotel Mohren Willisau / OM hört auf! Abschiedskonzert und 10-Jahr-Jubiläum (Hotel Mohren Willisau / OM Says Farewell! Farewell Concert and 10-Year Anniversary)
1982 Siebdruck – Screen print
128 × 90,5 cm

6 Missing Fukuda
2010 JP, FI Siebdruck – Screen print
128 × 90,5 cm

7 [Tote Bäume – Dead Trees]
1992 Siebdruck – Screen print
128 × 90,5 cm

8 Willisau Hotel Mohren / Jazz-Crew
1973 Siebdruck – Screen print
59,5 × 43 cm

9 Hotel Kreuz Willisau / Irène Schweizer / Buschi Niebergall / Allen Blairman
1973 Siebdruck – Screen print
60,5 × 45,5 cm

10 Willisau Mohren / Jazz Bass / Doppelkonzert mit Dave Holland Solo und dem Ron Carter Quartet (Willisau Mohren / Jazz Bass / Double Concert with Dave Holland Solo and the Ron Carter Quartet)
1981 Siebdruck – Screen print
128 × 90,5 cm

11 Hotel Mohren Willisau / Jazz in Willisau / George Coleman Quartet
1979 Siebdruck – Screen print
128 × 90,5 cm

12 Willisau Hotel Mohren / Don Pullen Quartet Featuring Chico Freeman Fred Hopkins Bobby Battle
1978 Siebdruck – Screen print
128 × 90,5 cm

13 Willisau Mohren / Sun Ra Arkestra
1980 Siebdruck – Screen print
128 × 90,5 cm

14 Hotel Mohren Willisau / Chris McGregor's Brotherhood of Breath
1973 Siebdruck – Screen print
60,5 × 39,5 cm

15 Willisau Hotel Kreuz / The New Anthony Braxton Quartet Featuring Ray Anderson Brian Smith Thurman Barker
1978 Siebdruck – Screen print
60 × 42 cm

16 Willisau Kanti-Aula / Keith Jarrett Trio / Keith Jarrett Charlie Haden Paul Motian
1972 Siebdruck – Screen print
60 × 38,5 cm

17 Jazz Festival Willisau '76
1976 Siebdruck – Screen print
128 × 90,5 cm

18 Jazz Festival Willisau '78
1978 Siebdruck – Screen print
128 × 90,5 cm

19 Jazz in Willisau / Foroom / Solo Vocals / Greetje Bijma
2004 Siebdruck – Screen print
128 × 90,5 cm

20 Jazz Festival Willisau '91
1991 Siebdruck – Screen print
128 × 90,5 cm

21 Willisau Stadtmühle / Lucien Dubuis Trio
2010 Siebdruck – Screen print
128 × 90,5 cm

22 Jazz in Willisau / Rathausbühne / Ellery Eskelin / Han Bennink
2000 Siebdruck – Screen print
128 × 90,5 cm

23 Jazz in Willisau / Rathausbühne / Jazz Italia / Carlo Actis Dato Quartet
2000 Siebdruck – Screen print
128 × 90,5 cm

24 Es guets Neus wünscht Bösch Siebdruck AG Stans (Ein gutes neues Jahr wünscht Bösch Siebdruck AG Stans – Bösch Siebdruck AG, Stans, Wishes You a Happy New Year)
2008 Siebdruck – Screen print
128 × 90,5 cm

25 Jazz Willisau / Foroom / Marty Ehrlich Quartet N. Y.
2006 Siebdruck – Screen print
128 × 90,5 cm

26 Willisau Rathaus / Kölner Saxophon Mafia
1999 Siebdruck – Screen print
128 × 90,5 cm

27 Jazz Willisau Foroom: Doppelmoppel / Gitarren: Uwe Kropinski und Helmut «Joe» Sachse / Posaunen: Konrad Bauer und Johannes Bauer (Jazz Willisau Foroom: Doppelmoppel / Guitar: Uwe Kropinski and Helmut "Joe" Sachse / Trombone: Konrad Bauer and Johannes Bauer)
2004 Siebdruck – Screen print
128 × 90,5 cm

28 Willisau Hotel Mohren / Doppelkonzert / Mike Osborne Quintet / Irène Schweizer Trio (Willisau Hotel Mohren / Double Concert / Mike Osborne Quintet / Irène Schweizer Trio)
1977 Siebdruck – Screen print
60 × 42 cm

29 Willisau Mohren / Cecil Taylor Solo
1989 Siebdruck – Screen print
128 × 90,5 cm

30 Niklaus Troxler / Jazz'n'more / Plakate / Museum Folkwang (Niklaus Troxler / Jazz'n'more / Posters / Museum Folkwang)
2017 DE Offset 84 × 59,5 cm

31 Willisau / American Indian Jazz & Dance / Jim Pepper's Pow Wow
1985 Siebdruck – Screen print
128 × 90,5 cm

32 Willisau Rathaus / Tim Berne's Paraphrase
1998 Siebdruck – Screen print
128 × 90,5 cm

33 Willisau Mohren / Brasil Jazz Night / Hermeto Pascoal e Grupo
1985 Siebdruck – Screen print
128 × 90,5 cm

34 Willisau Mohren / African Echoes / Doppelprogramm / Abdullah Ibrahim Dollar Brand / Pat Hall Smith – Warren Smith (Willisau Mohren / African Echoes / Double Concert / Abdullah Ibrahim Dollar Brand / Pat Hall Smith – Warren Smith)
1988 Siebdruck – Screen print
128 × 90,5 cm

35 Willisau Mohren / Jazz Meets India / Charlie Mariano & Karnataka College of Percussion Feat. R.A. Ramamani
1983 Siebdruck – Screen print
128 × 90,5 cm

36 Mohren / A Tribute to the Music of Thelonious Monk.
1986 Siebdruck – Screen print
128 × 90,5 cm

37 20 Jahre Kleintheater Luzern
(20 Years of Kleintheater Luzern)
1987 Siebdruck – Screen print
128 × 90,5 cm

38 Schluss mit der Schwarzmalerei!
Mut zur Wut. Plakataktion Heidelberg
2010. Niklaus Troxler (Enough of
that Doom and Gloom! Courage to
Rage. Poster Campaign Heidelberg
2010. Niklaus Troxler)
2010 DE Siebdruck – Screen print
118,5 × 84,5 cm

39 Willisau Mohren / Tania Maria
1988 Siebdruck – Screen print
128 × 90,5 cm

40 Willisau Hotel Mohren /
John Abercrombie / Dave Holland /
Jack DeJohnette
1975 Siebdruck – Screen print
60 × 39,5 cm

41 Hotel Mohren / Jazzkonzert
in Willisau / Willem Breuker Kollektief
1990 Siebdruck – Screen print
128 × 90,5 cm

42 Willisau Mohren / Bob Stewart
Group
1987 Siebdruck – Screen print
60 × 52,5 cm

43 Mohren / Jazz in Willisau /
Ray Anderson's Alligatory Band
1997 Siebdruck – Screen print
128 × 90,5 cm

44 Jazz in Willisau / Foroom /
Bob Stewart Tuba / Arthur Blythe
Alto Sax
2005 Siebdruck – Screen print
128 × 90,5 cm

45 SGV [Schweizer Grafiker
Verband] Generalversammlung /
Auf dem Menzberg bei Willisau
(SGV [Swiss Graphic Designers
Association] General Meeting /
At Menzberg Close to Willisau)
1989 Siebdruck – Screen print
128 × 90,5 cm

46 Kurtheater Baden /
Tribute to Fats Waller
1987 Siebdruck – Screen print
128 × 90,5 cm

47 Olma St. Gallen / Schweizer
Messe für Land- und Milchwirtschaft
(Olma St. Gallen / Swiss Trade Fair
for the Agriculture and Dairy Industry)
1994 Siebdruck – Screen print
128 × 90,5 cm

48 Landschaftstheater Ballenberg
'94 / Elsi, die seltsame Magd
(Landschaftstheater Ballenberg '94 /
Elsi, The Strange Maid)
1994 Siebdruck – Screen print
128 × 90,5 cm

49 Theatergesellschaft Willisau /
Die Spielverderber von Michael Ende
(Theatergesellschaft Willisau /
The Spoilsports by Michael Ende)
1994 Siebdruck – Screen print
128 × 90,5 cm

50 Ausstellung Schloss Lenzburg /
Die Welt der Anne Frank / Zeit-
geschichte – Aktualität – Bezüge
zur Schweiz (Schloss Lenzburg
Exhibition / The World of Anne Frank
/ Contemporary History – Present –
References to Switzerland)
1994 Siebdruck – Screen print
128 × 90,5 cm

51 Stadttheater Luzern / Otello /
Giuseppe Verdi
1991 Siebdruck – Screen print
128 × 90,5 cm

52 Willisau Rathaus / Keramik-
Ausstellung / Keramik-Forum Bern
(Willisau City Hall / Ceramics
Exhibition / Keramik-Forum Bern)
1994 Siebdruck – Screen print
128 × 90,5 cm

53 Im ehemaligen Schlachthaus
Zofingen / Das Lachen / nach dem
gleichnamigen Essay des französischen Philosophen Henri Bergson
(In the Former Zofingen Slaughter-
house / Laughter / based on an
essay of the same title by French
philosopher Henri Bergson)
1993 Siebdruck – Screen print
128 × 90,5 cm

54 Knie / Zürich Sechseläutenplatz
1981 Offset 128 × 271,5 cm

55 Hotel Mohren / Jazz in Willisau /
Joe McPhee Trio
1975 Siebdruck – Screen print
60,5 × 42 cm

56 Willisau Mohren /
Keith Jarrett Quartet
1976 Siebdruck – Screen print
60 × 42 cm

57 Hotel Kreuz Willisau /
Stu Martin / Drums & Synthesizer
1973 Siebdruck – Screen print
60 × 43,5 cm

58 Willisau Stadtmühle /
Uli Kempendorff & Friends
2014 Siebdruck – Screen print
128 × 90,5 cm

59 Rathaus Willisau /
David Murray Solo
2001 Siebdruck – Screen print
128 × 90.5 cm

60 Willisau Hotel Mohren / The Trio /
John Surman / Barre Phillips /
Stu Martin
1976 Siebdruck – Screen print
60,5 × 42 cm

61 Willisau Mohren / Arthur
Blythe Quartet Feat. Abdul Wadud,
Bob Stewart, Bobby Battle
1982 Siebdruck – Screen print
128 × 90,5 cm

62 Blues in Willisau / Kreuzstube /
Champion Jack Dupree
1970 Siebdruck – Screen print
52 × 32,5 cm

63 Willisau Rathaus /
Kenny Wheeler Quartet
2001 Siebdruck – Screen print
128 × 90,5 cm

64 Jazz in Willisau / Kreuzstube /
Pierre-Favre-Trio Meets Trevor Watts
as England
1970 Siebdruck – Screen print
64 × 45 cm

65 Willisau Hotel Kreuz /
The Michal-Urbaniak-Group
1971 Siebdruck – Screen print
60 × 41 cm

66 Jazz in Willisau / Mohren /
Fred Wesley Group
1992 Siebdruck – Screen print
128 × 90,5 cm

67 Willisau / Rathaus Parterre /
Echoes of Techno / Wolfgang
Muthspiel / Christian Muthspiel
2000 Siebdruck – Screen print
128,5 × 90,5 cm

68 Jazz im Bau 4 Altbüron /
OM / Christy Doran / Bobby Burri /
Urs Leimgruber / Fredy Studer
2016 Siebdruck – Screen print
128 × 90,5 cm

69 Jazz im Bau 4 Altbüron /
The Workers / Urs Leimgruber /
Omri Ziegele / Christian Weber /
Alex Huber
2019 Siebdruck – Screen print
128 × 90,5 cm

70 Willisau Mohren /
Maria João Vocal / Aki Takase Piano
1988 Siebdruck – Screen print
128 × 90,5 cm

71 Jazz im Bau 4 Altbüron /
Luca Sisera / Roofer
2020 Siebdruck – Screen print
128 × 90,5 cm

72 Theatergesellschaft Willisau /
Drei Mal Leben von Yasmina Reza
(Theatergesellschaft Willisau /
Life × 3 by Yasmina Reza)
2005 Siebdruck – Screen print
128 × 90,5 cm

73 Jazz in Willisau / Foroom /
Jim Black & Alas No Axis / Jim Black /
Chris Speed / Skuli Sverisson /
Hilmar Jensson
2006 Siebdruck – Screen print
128 × 90,5 cm

74 Jazz im Bau 4 Altbüron /
Skein Quartet / Frank Gratkowski /
Achim Kaufmann / Wilbert de
Joode / Tony Buck
2018 Digitaldruck – Digital print
128 × 90,5 cm

75 Public / Niklaus Troxler
for Public Bikes Inc., San Francisco
2012 US Siebdruck – Screen print
128 × 90,5 cm

76 Jazz in Willisau / Foroom /
Amina Claudine Myers Solo
2008 Siebdruck – Screen print
128 × 90,5 cm

77 Jazz in Willisau / Rathausbühne /
BassDrumBone / Mark Helias /
Gerry Hemingway / Ray Anderson
1999 Siebdruck – Screen print
128 × 90,5 cm

78 Jazz in Willisau im neuen Club
Foroom / Christy Doran's New Bag /
CD-Taufe und Club Opening (Jazz
in Willisau in the New Club Foroom /
Christy Doran's New Bag / CD
Launch and Club Opening)
2002 Siebdruck – Screen print
128 × 90,5 cm

79 Jazz Willisau / Foroom /
Charles Gayle Solo
2009 Siebdruck – Screen print
128 × 90,5 cm

80 Jazzconcert Willisau im Foroom /
The Ellery Eskelin Trio
2007 Siebdruck – Screen print
128 × 90,5 cm

81 Jazz in Willisau / Foroom /
Simon Nabatov / Piano Solo
2003 Siebdruck – Screen print
128 × 90,5 cm

82 Ausstellung im Rathaus Willisau /
Typo Plakate (Exhibition at
the Willisau City Hall / Typographic
Posters)
1996 Siebdruck – Screen print
128 × 90,5 cm

83 If You Cover Helvetica It Looks
Quite Nice / Helvetica 50 Years
(Wenn man die Helvetica abdeckt,
sieht sie ganz nett aus / 50 Jahre
Helvetica)
2007 Siebdruck – Screen print
128 × 90,5 cm

84 Eine offene Schweiz, s.v.p.!
(An Open Switzerland, s.v.p.!)
2016 Siebdruck – Screen print
128 × 90,5 cm

85 Stiftung Sonneschyn Luzern.
Hilfe für das sexuell ausgebeutete
Kind (Stiftung Sonneschyn Luzern.
Support for Sexually Exploited
Children)
1997 Siebdruck – Screen print
128 × 271,5 cm

86 Gewalt! Halt! (Violence! Stop!)
1993 Siebdruck – Screen print
128 × 271,5 cm

87 [CH – EU]
1996 Siebdruck – Screen print
128 × 90,5 cm

88 Demo Crazy
2021 Digitaldruck – Digital print
128 × 90,5 cm

89 Steuerflu[ch]t / Niklaus Troxler /
Mut zur Wut / Plakataktion Heidelberg 2013 (Tax Evasion / Niklaus
Troxler / Courage to Rage / Poster
Campaign Heidelberg 2013)
2013 DE Siebdruck – Screen print
128 × 90,5 cm

90 Augen auf / Ohren auf /
Mund auf (Eyes Open / Ears Open /
Mouth Open)
2021 Digitaldruck – Digital print
128 × 90,5 cm

91 WWF / For a Living Planet
(WWF / Für einen lebenden Planeten)
2005 Siebdruck – Screen print
128 × 90,5 cm

92 Schlussfeier in Basel /
700 Jahre Eidgenossenschaft
(Final Celebration in Basel /
700 Years of the Confederation)
1991 Siebdruck – Screen print
171,5 × 120 cm

93 61e Salon de l'Auto et
Accessoires Genève / Palexpo
1991 Siebdruck – Screen print
128 × 90,5 cm

94 Ouverture du 700ème /
Bellinzona (Eröffnung der
700-Jahrfeier – Opening of the
700th Anniversary)
1991 Siebdruck – Screen print
128 × 90,5 cm

95 Fest der vier Kulturen /
Französische Schweiz / Utopien /
700 Jahre Eidgenossenschaft
(Festival of the Four Cultures /
French-Speaking Switzerland /
Utopias / 700 Years of the
Confederation)
1991 Siebdruck – Screen print
128 × 90,5 cm
(aus einer dreiteiligen Plakat-
kampagne – from a three-part poster
campaign)

96 Olma St. Gallen / Schweizer
Messe für Land- und Milchwirtschaft
(Olma St. Gallen / Swiss Trade
Fair for the Agriculture and Dairy
Industry)
1988 Offset 128 × 90,5 cm

97 Vaterland / Die Zeitung mit Linie /
Jetzt mit farbigem TV-Magazin
(Vaterland / The Newspaper with
Clear Lines / Now With a Color TV
Supplement)
1991 Siebdruck – Screen print
128 × 90,5 cm
(aus einer mehrteiligen Plakat-
kampagne – from a multi-part poster
campaign)

98–100 Vaterland / Die Zeitung mit
Linie (Vaterland / The Newspaper
With Clear Lines)
1989 Siebdruck – Screen print
128 × 90,5 cm
(aus einer mehrteiligen Plakat-
kampagne – from a multi-part poster
campaign)

101 Sörenberg-Flühli
2015 Digitaldruck – Digital print
128 × 90,5 cm

102 Jazz in Willisau / Rathaus /
Gianluigi Trovesi / Gianni Coscia Duo
1999 Siebdruck – Screen print
128 × 271,5 cm

103 Jazz in Willisau / Foroom /
Baby Sommer / Greek Connection
2008 Siebdruck – Screen print
128 × 90,5 cm

104 Bau 4 Altbüron / Tape & Jazz /
Niklaus Troxler Live Taping
2021 Siebdruck – Screen print
128 × 90,5 cm

105 Jazz Festival Willisau '08
2008 Siebdruck – Screen print
128 × 271,5 cm

106 Jazz Festival Willisau 97
1997 Siebdruck – Screen print
128 × 271,5 cm

107 Jazz im Bau 4, Altbüron /
Tree Ear. Sebastian Stinning, Gerry
Hemingway, Manuel Troller
2016 Siebdruck – Screen print
128 × 90,5 cm

108 Jazz in Willisau / Rathaus /
Solo Guitar Recital / Uwe Kropinski
1998 Siebdruck – Screen print
128 × 271,5 cm

109 Jazz im Bau 4, Altbüron /
The Samuel Blaser Quartet /
Samuel Blaser / Russ Lossing /
Masa Kamaguchi / Gerry Hemingway
2019 Siebdruck – Screen print
128 × 90,5 cm

Ausgewählte Literatur / Selected Bibliography

Alperson, Philip, «On Musical Improvisation», in:
The Journal of Aesthetics and Art Criticism 43 (1984),
pp. 17–29.

Diederichsen, Diedrich, *Über Pop-Musik,* Köln 2014.

Döring, Jürgen, «Niklaus Troxler», in: *Plakatkunst
von Toulouse-Lautrec bis Benetton,* exhib. cat., Museum
für Kunst und Gewerbe Hamburg, Hamburg 1994,
pp. 200–201.

Feige, Daniel Martin, *Design. Eine philosophische Analyse*,
Berlin 2018.

Feige, Daniel Martin, *Philosophie des Jazz,* Berlin 2014.

Ginza Graphic Gallery (ed.), *Niklaus Troxler,* Tokyo 2007.

Gracyk, Theodore, Andrew Kania (eds.), *The Routledge
Companion to Philosophy and Music,* London 2011.

He, Jianping (ed.), *Troxler,* «Master of Design» series,
Singapore 2007.

Jubert, Roxane (ed.), *Niklaus Troxler,* Design & Designer
54, Paris 2007.

Kivy, Peter, *Introduction to a Philosophy of Music,*
Oxford 2002.

Niklaus Troxler. Jazz'n'more – Plakate, exhib. cat.,
Museum Folkwang Essen, Göttingen 2017.

Odermatt, Siegfried, «Niklaus Troxler», in: *100 + 3
Schweizer Plakate ausgewählt von Siegfried Odermatt,*
Zürich 1998, pp. 150–151.

Troxler, Niklaus, Olivier Senn, *Willisau and All That Jazz,*
Bern 2013.

Troxler, Niklaus (ed.), *Jazz Blvd.: Niklaus Troxler, Posters,*
Baden 1999.

Wilson, Peter Niklas, Walter Lachenmann (eds.),
*Niklaus Troxler: Jazzplakate / Jazz Posters / Affiches
de Jazz,* Schaftlach 1991.

www.troxlerart.ch

www.willisaujazzarchive.ch/posters

Autoren / Authors

Bettina Richter

Geboren 1964, Kunsthistorikerin. 1996 Dissertation über die Antikriegsgrafiken von Théophile-Alexandre Steinlen. 1997–2006 wissenschaftliche Mitarbeiterin in der Plakatsammlung des Museum für Gestaltung Zürich. Seit 2006 Kuratorin der Plakatsammlung. Nebenbei Tätigkeit als Dozentin an der Zürcher Hochschule der Künste sowie als freischaffende Autorin.

Born in 1964, art historian. 1996 dissertation on the antiwar graphics of Théophile-Alexandre Steinlen. From 1997 to 2006, served as a research associate for the Poster Collection of the Museum für Gestaltung Zürich, since 2006 as its curator. Also lectures at the Zurich University of the Arts and works as a freelance writer.

Daniel Martin Feige

Professor für Philosophie und Ästhetik in der Fachgruppe Design an der Staatlichen Akademie der Bildenden Künste Stuttgart. Promotion an der Goethe-Universität in Frankfurt (mit einer Arbeit zu Hegels Kunstphilosophie), Habilitation mit Studien zur Ästhetik 2017 an der Freien Universität Berlin. Er forscht und veröffentlicht an der Schnittstelle von Themen der philosophischen Ästhetik sowie der theoretischen und praktischen Philosophie. Jüngste Monografien: *Die Natur des Menschen. Eine dialektische Anthropologie* (Berlin 2022); *Musik für Designer* (Stuttgart 2021); *Design. Eine philosophische Analyse* (Berlin 2018).

Daniel Martin Feige is a professor of philosophy and aesthetics with a special focus on design at the Stuttgart State Academy of Art and Design. He earned his doctorate at Goethe University in Frankfurt with a dissertation on Hegel's philosophy of art, and in 2017 completed his habilitation in aesthetics at the Free University Berlin. He researches and publishes at the intersection of philosophical aesthetics and theoretical and practical philosophy. Recent monographs include *Die Natur des Menschen: Eine dialektische Anthropologie* (Berlin 2022); *Musik für Designer* (Stuttgart 2021); and *Design: Eine philosophische Analyse* (Berlin 2018).

Dank / Acknowledgments

Publikations- und Ausstellungsprojekte sind immer ein willkommener Anlass, den eigenen umfangreichen Bestand an Plakaten themenspezifisch zu sichten, aufzuarbeiten und zu ergänzen. Dank der regelmässigen Donationen von Niklaus Troxler konnten wir auf seine zahlreichen Plakate im Bestand der Plakatsammlung des Museum für Gestaltung Zürich zurückgreifen. Im Zusammenhang mit der vorliegenden Publikation hat Niklaus Troxler der Sammlung weitere Plakate geschenkt. Wir danken Niklaus Troxler zudem für intensive Gespräche und Auskünfte zu seinem Schaffen.

Publication and exhibition projects are always welcome occasions to examine and work with our own extensive holdings of posters with a specific theme in mind, and also to update it with targeted acquisitions. In preparing this publication we have drawn on numerous posters by Niklaus Troxler, who is already well represented in the Poster Collection of the Museum für Gestaltung Zürich. This is largely due to regular donations of work by the designer himself. In connection with the present publication, he has donated further posters to the collection. We would also like to thank Niklaus Troxler for engaging in an intensive dialogue with us and sharing information about his work.

Museum für Gestaltung Zürich

Eine Publikation des Museum für Gestaltung Zürich
Christian Brändle, Direktor

A Publication of the Museum für Gestaltung Zürich
Christian Brändle, Director

Niklaus Troxler
Konzept und Redaktion / Concept and editing: Bettina Richter,
Petra Schmid, Barbara Schenkel
Gestaltung / Design: Integral Lars Müller
Übersetzung / Translation: Susan Ring (Ger.–Eng.)
Lektorat Deutsch / German copyediting: Markus Zehentbauer
Lektorat Englisch / English copyediting: Adam Blauhut
Fotografie / Photography: Ivan Šuta
Lithografie / Repro: prints professional, Berlin, Germany
Druck, Einband / Printing, binding: Belvédère, Oosterbeek,
the Netherlands

Reihe / Series «Poster Collection»
Herausgegeben von / Edited by
Museum für Gestaltung Zürich, Plakatsammlung
Bettina Richter, Kuratorin der Plakatsammlung /
Curator of the Poster Collection
In Zusammenarbeit mit / In cooperation with
Petra Schmid, Publikationen / Publications
Museum für Gestaltung Zürich

The museum of
Zurich University of the Arts
zhdk.ch

Museum für Gestaltung Zürich
Ausstellungsstrasse 60
Postfach
8031 Zürich, Switzerland
www.museum-gestaltung.ch

Museum für Gestaltung Zürich
Plakatsammlung / Poster Collection
sammlungen@museum-gestaltung.ch

Lars Müller Publishers
8005 Zürich, Switzerland
www.lars-mueller-publishers.com

ISBN 978-3-03778-687-1
Erste Auflage / First edition

Printed in the Netherlands

Wir danken für Unterstützung /
For their support we thank:

POSTER COLLECTION

01 REVUE 1926

02 DONALD BRUN

03 POSTERS FOR EXHIBITIONS 1980–2000

04 HORS-SOL

05 TYPOTECTURE

06 VISUAL STRATEGIES AGAINST AIDS

07 ARMIN HOFMANN

08 BLACK AND WHITE

09 RALPH SCHRAIVOGEL

10 MICHAEL ENGELMANN

11 HANDMADE

12 CATHERINE ZASK

13 TYPO CHINA

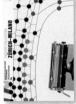
14 ZÜRICH–MILANO

15 BREAKING THE RULES

16 COMIX!

17 PHOTO GRAPHICS

18 OTTO BAUMBERGER

19 HEAD TO HEAD

20 HELP!

21 PARADISE SWITZERLAND

22 LETTERS ONLY

23 IN SERIES

24 THE MAGIC OF THINGS

25 JOSEF MÜLLER-BROCKMANN

26 JAPAN–NIPPON

27 THE HAND

28 HERBERT LEUPIN

29 HAMBURGER–STAEHELIN

30 SELF-PROMOTION

31 STOP MOTION

32 EN VOGUE

33 JA! NEIN! YES! NO! SWISS POSTERS FOR DEMOCRACY